Dedicated to Nell,
Co-Editor of My Life,
And to Our First Issues, Charles, Meredith, & Nathaniel

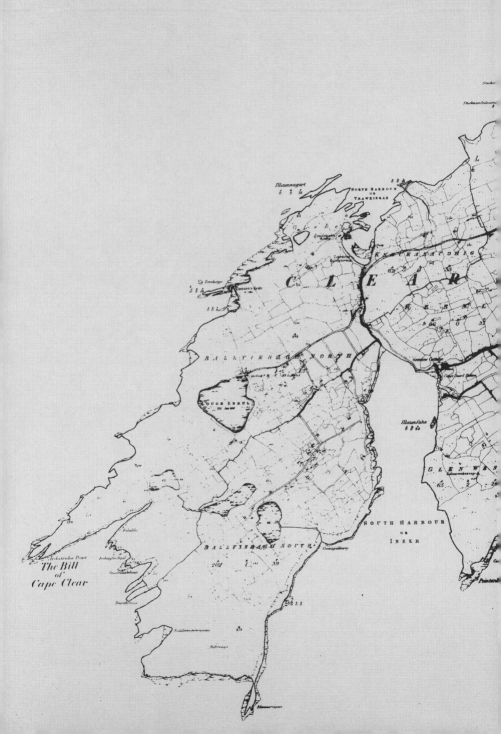

Cape Clear
Island Magic

*A Photographic, Historical & Dramatic Account of
Clear Island, Ireland*

By Chuck Kruger

THE COLLINS PRESS

Published by
The Collins Press, Carey's Lane, Cork.

Text © Chuck Kruger 1994.

Printed in Ireland by
Colour Books Ltd., Dublin.

Book Design by Upper Case Ltd., Cork
Typeset by Upper Case Ltd., Cork.

ISBN 1898256012

Contents

About the Author

Born in 1938, Chuck Kruger grew up in the Finger Lakes Region of New York State. He studied literature at Hamilton College (BA) and Washington University (MA), and psychology at the C. G. Jung Institut, Switzerland. He worked as a teacher, counselor and lecturer in Philadelphia, St. Louis, and Zurich, where he lived for 26 years. In 1986 he and his wife Nell purchased a farm on Clear Island, County Cork, where they moved in 1992. Turned full-time freelance writer and poet at 53, he regularly contributes feature articles to *The Cork Examiner* and various magazines in Switzerland and the US, has read some of his pieces on RTE's "Sunday Miscellany", has co-edited a Spring Publications book entitled *Shadow and Evil in Fairy Tales*. Father of three grown children, he's presently completing a children's book about St. Ciaran, Clear Island's patron saint, a collection of short stories and a book entitled *Growing Up in the USA*. Of his adopted island he says: "Cape's a poem I read every day, every night. It's a point of reference, a metaphor by which I confirm my very being. It's the place I love more than any other."

ACKNOWLEDGMENTS

Special thanks to Sean Dunne and Tony O'Mahony, whose encouragement led to the publication of versions of many chapters that follow in *The Cork Examiner's Weekend* and *West Cork News* to Paraic O'Neil and Lorelei Harris, producers of RTE's radio program "Sunday Miscellany", on which condensations of chapters have been broadcast; to the American magazine ISLANDS and the Swiss magazine ORNIS, in which versions of "Summer's Day" and "Birds", respectively, have been published; to Island Trust's magazine "An t-Oileánach", where sections of chapters have appeared; to Dave Bird, Richard Humpidge and Clive Hutchinson for their ornithological advice; to Paddy O'Leary for sharing his archaeological knowledge and discovery with me; to Kate Sawyer, for allowing me to publish several of her photographs; to the staff at the Skibbereen library, who have generously located books; to Mrs. Kieran Cotter, for permission to publish several photographs from her family's collection; to Pierce Hickey, for his photographic advice and assistance; to my neighbours and friends on Cape, who have shared lore and stories, and who have kindly allowed me to ramble every rabbit track, prowl every field, and have shown humorously stoic patience with all my questions and curiosities; to the Ordnance Survey for permission to reprint their maps (Government Permit No. 5826); and to my wife Nell, without whose tolerance of my ways — grammatical, aesthetic, and gustatory — and without whose loving red pen this book would not, could not, have been written.

Foreword

The long hump of Cape Clear rose out of the sea like a blowing whale ....

Peter Somerville-Large's *The Coast of West Cork*

A convert to Cape, I'm what the locals call a "blow-in": I've blown in from somewhere else like a seed on the wind, with the implication that I could, tomorrow, just as easily blow on to somewhere else. But I'm afraid that Cape's stuck with me, for I experience myself putting down roots into this rough sandstone island "promontory", as it was referred to hundreds of years back. Whether I'm the toxic ragwort, the encroaching fern (bracken), the gentle Joseph's Ladder — the regional name for Montbretia — or something that hasn't grown here before and that won't upset the ecological balance, this book will make the determination clear, Cape clear.

As an outsider to Ireland as well as to Cape, my perspective has advantages and disadvantages: I see landscapes, customs, history, even weather as if for the first time. Thus I can respond enthusiastically but also naively, objectively but also blindly, subjectively. While free of some cultural collective biases, I'm also imprisoned by those I bring with me. Without Irish, I'm often at a loss when islanders try to share place names, anecdotes and stories with me. Thus, to communicate Cape to you, I rely not merely on compiled library research, but on photographs, poems, short stories, lore gained first-hand through conversations in pastures and pubs, tales heard while lobstering or building a house or mailing letters or climbing a stile. I try, then, to present Cape not only from the head, but from the eye, the heart. As a consequence, I vary my style from chapter to chapter and sometimes, as when a personal approach will dramatise or clarify Cape better than statistics or bald facts, within chapters.

People ask how I came to Cape in the first place; others ask —

The long hump of Cape.

especially when a strong gale has been howling like a banshee about the gables for a week straight — why I stay; still others ask why I left comfy Switzerland after twenty-six years there. The following part of this foreword serves as an introduction to Cape, to me, and to my sometimes anecdotal style.

Cut off from the mainland by eight treacherous sea-miles of sudden rock and powerful tidal currents, exposed to the ripping wind from every direction, sometimes covered by salt and foam, practically devoid of sheltering trees, stony and hilly, without major stores or services, downright isolated, a last outpost, Clear Island, County Cork, Ireland, called us — my wife Nell and me — away from our secure quiet home in Switzerland. There we might have boasted a peaceful view of lake and mountains and castle, proximity to field and vineyard and forest, easy quick access to what some refer to as high civilisation: fabulous hospitals, universities, ski slopes, concert halls, opera house, indoor tennis and squash, a variety of ethnic restaurants, people from all over the world, Joyce's Zurich a Dublin without poverty, the countryside clipped and pruned and as ordered as a beloved kitchen garden. So why, Cape neighbors ask, do you want to live here? How did you happen to find us? Just how crazy are you?

We first visited Ireland in 1979, returned to Switzerland convinced that, yes, rural Ireland still had a quality of living that we believed made it the most friendly country we had ever toured. Totally pleased with our vacation, we went back to teaching, wondering if another year we would journey to Israel or to Spain.

St. Ciaran's Cemetery.

Not until 1986 did we think of Ireland again, after looking at the photographs we had taken in '79. I especially remember one showing a deserted thatched cottage (somewhere south of Valentia) that had a riot of foxglove growing randomly on the thatched roof; the fog obscured the background. Then we came upon an old French tourist magazine with a two-page spread, an aerial photograph of the quaint village of Baltimore, with Sherkin Island resplendently verdant behind it, and a touch of something else out at sea.

The spring and early summer of 1986 friends began to arrive in Switzerland, one group after another, and we began to experience our tiny home as a busy B&B, Nell the cook and me the bottle-washer. While we enjoyed our friends individually — collectively, sequentially, they overwhelmed us: so when we saw two weeks without visitors ahead, we packed our knapsacks before anyone else could arrive. Two days after the idea hit we were hitchhiking in the boiling sun from Cork airport in the direction of Baltimore. We had meant to rent bikes, but the day was a scorcher, Cork was to the east, and we wanted to mosey west, so that was that. In our late forties, we hitchhiked for the first time since our early twenties. A priest picked us up, then a farmer, an insurance man, an elderly artist, grandparents with two young children. Three hours later we were in Baltimore, wandering about and feeling that here was a gentle, honest, one-street town, with a thriving low-key kid-centered harbour, but not quite what we were looking for. Sherkin called.

For three days we tramped Sherkin. One place caught our fancy, a small headland that shot due south, with, we romanticised, nothing between it and the South Pole. Every day we picnicked there, rain or shine, watching the breaking waves and feeling the need to stare emptily out into the sea, and to something shadowy to the southeast. After three days, despite the magnificent Horseshoe Harbour, the charm of the Franciscan Friary, and the enthrallment we felt on that point, we were thankful we'd gone to Sherkin but ready to leave. We thought, Achill Island next!

Safely back in Baltimore, we hoisted our packs and were about to set forth thumbing when we saw a land auctioneer's sign, and decided — as far as one can decide to do anything — to go meet him and tell him in all innocence and silliness that if that point ever came up for sale in five years, to let us know. The auctioneer wanted to know what we liked about it, we talked, and finally he said, "I know a piece of land out on Cape, and I think it might be quite like the headland on Sherkin, though a little larger. I'm going in to Cape on the 2:15 mailboat with my wife and mother-in-law; join me if you like; I'll show you the property. And if you decide not to go, good luck to ye and no harm done."

At 2:15 we sailed on the *Naomh Ciaran*, left Sherkin astern, and instead of hiking toward places north, were steaming south toward what our guide books suggested was a haven for those twenty years our junior, what with a youth hostel and a camp site, and bird watchers galore. How impulsive we felt.

And then something happened, something magical, something for

Ballyieragh.

Open-air Mass, North Harbour.

which islands are renowned. I was on the starboard side swapping sailing yarns with our gregarious auctioneer; Nell was on the port side exchanging bringing-up-children stories with his wife and mother. As we entered North Harbour I chanced to look up, and there was a picturesque twelfth-century ruin of a chapel, beside it a stark homely cemetery, at the head of the harbour a holy well, and, in the middle of hearing a yachtsman's tale, I felt a rush of feeling come over me, my eyes wet, I had an ebullient sense that here, dead ahead, was a place where I could die. I brushed my tears with my sleeve so that he, perhaps, wouldn't notice anything amiss, and went on listening to his tale.

A few months later, back in Switzerland at a small dinner party, life savings now into the unexpected purchase of an island property, someone asked me how I knew Cape was where I wanted to be, and I told the story of my first entry to North Harbour. Nell looked at me, not having heard my story before, and told hers. She, she said, happened to look up as we entered North Harbour, saw a crumbling chapel, saw the modest graveyard, the Virgin Mary statue by the well, and felt a rush of feeling come over her, bringing tears to her eyes: she knew that here was a place she could die happily. She went back to listening to a story about bringing up fourteen-year-olds.

I should add that neither of us is particularly anxious to die, nor are we particularly lachrymose. But having lived in Switzerland for all of those years, we failed to develop any sense of connection to its earth. Somehow, for us, the very order of the country killed its spirit. We don't like park benches in the middle of woods or on mountain tops, nor doggie-do boxes with plastic bags at the ready alongside a country road. It's too civilised by half. We prefer raggedy Ireland to manicured Helvetica.

Some live wherever they happen to be or to have been brought up, some choose their location, and a few have no choice but to go to where they are called. My wife and I have discovered we have no choice, for better or for worse. So that's our story of how we found Cape — or, perhaps, of how it found us.

Chapter One
Background

I thought," he said, "that the Island wasn't half as big as it is."
"Ambasa," said I, "it is much larger than one would ever conceive."
Conchúr O Síocháin's *The Man from Cape Clear*

Clear Island, the southernmost inhabited land off the Irish coast, may be small in size — a mere three miles long by one mile wide — but large in history and picturesque scenery. Physicists theorise that a piece of matter the size of a fist could have the weight of the entire earth; Cape has that kind of density, but in an aesthetic sense. The more one comes to know the island, the more — miraculously — there is to know.

To reach this rugged, more insular than isolated island, one boards in Baltimore the state-subsidised *Naomh Ciaran II*, which runs one of two eight-mile routes at least once a day year round (gales permitting, and barring Christmas day). Arriving at North Harbour forty-five minutes later, returning

Croha West standing stone.

1

locals are, as the idiom has it, now "in", having been "out", or visiting that country called Ireland.

Island antiquities include Neolithic and Bronze Age standing stones, a passage tomb with the only summer solstice alignment in County Cork (see Chapter III for an account of the national and international significance of this tomb), an alleged ogham stone, a boulder burial (which used to be called a dolmen, or a boulder dolmen), a prehistoric cooking site (*fulacht fiadh*). Unauthenticated wedge-tombs, souterrains and hut foundations, which appear on no archeological maps, await authentication and analysis, as do possible ringforts. A replica of the inscribed Cape Clear Stone, which scholars often compare to stones from Newgrange, and photographs of some of the other ancient stones, may be viewed in the island's Heritage Centre.

Other antiquities include Bronze Age mines; St. Kieran's Pillar Stone, the cross on which legend attributes to the saint himself, thus placing the reworked Celtic stone in the 4th to 5th century A.D.; the Romanesque St. Ciaran's Church (erected in the 12th or 13th century on the site of earlier structures), now a ruin; the 13th to 15th century O'Driscoll Castle (see Chapter IV), also a ruin since a cannonball attack in 1601; a British signal tower and garrison constructed in Napoleonic days; an abandoned lighthouse (of still unblemished Cornish granite ashlars) assembled in 1817-18; the Telegraph House, built in the 1850's; the Coastguard Station and Protestant Rectory (now the Youth Hostel), built about a decade earlier.

Then there are the sheer cliffs rising several hundred feet, a knoll beside the windmills 533 feet high (from which one can view both north and south sides of the island), a freshwater lake, reed-covered bogs, miniature hidden harbours, blowholes, sea caves (some hundreds of feet long), stacks, small streams, beaches, vantage points for whale and dolphin and seabird watching, miles and miles of walking paths, lonely sailors' graves, massive patches of lichen and wild flowers.

One should also mention the bird observatory with hostel and warden, the museum, three pubs, a fish farm, small grocery stores, a restaurant, craft stores, Protestant and Catholic cemeteries, a Catholic Church (with resident priest), a camp site and a youth hostel on the shore of the mile-long unspoilt South Harbour.

And everywhere one sees the quiet patchwork of over 1600 small fields divided by dry stone walls, the stone ruins of houses from days past, vistas of the distant Mizen Head, of Roaringwater Bay, of the mountains of West Cork, including Mount Gabriel and the often

2

Cloch na Geallúna (on left).

cloud-capped Hungry Hill, all defined and redefined by ever-shifting light and atmosphere. Herds of cattle, sometimes with a goat or two in the midst, graze the pastures. Here and there a donkey or horse cross-grazes the land. Rabbits abound. So do cats and dogs, chickens and guinea fowl. I know but a single peacock. Occasionally one may spot a sea otter. All this on — sources vary — 1578 acres.

In summer the island population swells from its 140 permanent inhabitants to as many as 500, not including day-trippers. Two summer colleges attract Irish youth intent on polishing their Irish and experiencing a Gaeltacht area. Yachts arrive not only from Kinsale and Dublin, but from England, France, Sweden, the United States, and often moor for a few days in one of the two main harbours. On a summer bank holiday weekend as many as one hundred tents may dot the campsite. Day-trippers from the mainland, departing from Schull and from Baltimore, walk the hilly meandering roads, bask in the sun alongside the harbours, picnic on some upland rock, snooze in a snug heathery niche.

On quiet days, which most summer days are, canoe (kayak) lessons are provided to college students, island youth and visitors. Most evenings music, spontaneous or hired, can be heard in the pubs; often of a Saturday or Sunday afternoon a "session" will occur in Cotter's Yard or in front of Paddy Burke's Pub or beside the Club. On regatta days, and Baltimore Lifeboat days, North Harbour fills with yachts and people. As many as a hundred yachts have sailed in the Cape Clear Regatta, a fun race held annually, with prizes going to the slowest boat, to the boat from furthest away, to the boat that didn't race, as well as to the winner. Set dancing, raffles, and traditional music provide active entertainment.

While Cape's future remains uncertain, significant changes wrought over the last 30-odd years may well have halted the depopulation trend of the previous 150 years, partly by attracting to the Gaeltacht island students and tourists who spend money on goods and services, partly by improving the standard of living, partly by making nontraditional ways of earning a living possible. These changes include: the establishment of two Irish colleges, the Co-op (which oversees the running of the ferry, the petrol pump, the electricity system, delivery of coal and cooking gas, renting of heavy equipment, and one of the colleges), the Bird Observatory (ornithologists report that Cape is perhaps the best place for birdwatching in all of Ireland), the Youth Hostel, the pottery, the fish farm, a small cluster of holiday homes, island-wide macadamised roads, thus allowing cars and tractors, JCB's and diggers, electricity generated both by windmills and by diesel and water storage tanks supplying customers by gravity-feed.

In this cottage industry/electronic age one no longer needs to live in the centre of a town or city to be gainfully employed at occupations other than farming and fishing. The island too is going high tech: it now has satellite dish antennas, computers, faxes, photocopy machines, fifty-five telephones, almost as many televisions and VCR's. Indeed, reliable electricity, and the high tech it allows, may enable Cape to attract new settlers to its community, thus assuring its viability.

Traditional island occupations, fishing and farming, continue to occupy people, but mostly on a part-time or supplemental basis. Only one fishing vessel, the *Ard Casta*, goes out from the island for more than a day at a time, usually six days at a stretch. With a complement of 3 on board, one ship doesn't make Cape — which, according to T.G. Green, in 1920 had a fleet of of 43 fishing boats employing 209 — a base for the fishing industry. Other islanders fish directly from Cape, but in open boats in fair weather, usually for lobster with a string or two of ten to twenty pots. One person collects and sells periwinkle. A handful shoot the occasional mackerel or herring net.

Four other islanders fish full-time, but not directly from the island. To be competitive in the fishing industry, it appears that most must operate from a major port, with transportation, ice and support facilities at the ready. For now, the "floating fish factory" ships, which vacuum the seas, and the large trawlers are winning, making margins so small, and capital investment so great, that few fishermen from places like Cape can compete.

If one wants to set up as a successful farmer, one doesn't normally decide to move to an often wind-swept, sometimes salt-burnt, occasionally unreachable, rocky island without a vet in residence, without arable fields of any size (a three-acre field, called *Gort Mor* — The Big Field — is said to be one of the largest fertile plots on Cape), without much topsoil in the majority of the fields. Consequently not many young couples, about to commit themselves to taking out a mortgage and to rearing a family, are prepared to settle on Cape, and a comparatively short time later see their children shipped off to boarding school at the age of 12. The island, then, has not been able to attract young farmers and fishermen to settle there, nor has it been able to provide employment for most of its own maturing youth. This fact could account for half of Cape's farmers, both full- and part-time, being over 60.

I can't think of one family which relies solely on farming for its entire income. Most island men supplement their farming by fishing, hauling, building, bartending, working for the County Council, the Post Office, the Co-op, the mailboat. As with the fishing industry, it's difficult to compete with the mainland with any degree of financial success. Mainland farmers can plough more than ten acres without having to back up once or squeeze through one gate or gap; they can have all deliveries of seed or feed or building blocks or cement made right to the barn door; they can have woodland protection for delicate crops, and mountains and miles of land to absorb the brunt of Atlantic storms. Then it's no wonder islanders have to juggle different ways of livelihood. To emend the proverb, Cape islanders are jacks of many trades, masters of most.

Cape women too juggle a multitude of jobs, including farming, running B&B's and self-catering establishments, managing craft stores and one of the small grocery stores, potting, delivering mail, caring for Irish college students, working as publicans, teachers, Co-op secretary, resident nurse.

Before I determined to move permanently to Cape, I asked many islanders, men and women, what advice they would have for me. The consensus: Learn to do things for yourself, to be independent, self-

5

reliant; then you will survive the rigours of the island — and be able to appreciate its peace.

Chapter Two
The Seasons,
The People

... [Cape] is separated from the mainland by the sound of Gaskenane, in which is always a strong tide, and in high winds a very heavy sea; and having, consequently, less intercourse with it than the islands nearer the coast, the native inhabitants have retained more of their original manners, language, and customs.

Samuel Lewis's *Topographical Dictionary of Ireland*, 1837

Cape's not only an island of variety but of stark contrasts, and not only from minute to minute — as when you witness half a dozen rainbows of an April afternoon — but from season to season, century to century. Compare its peak population of 1800 to 2000 in the 18th century with its 140 today; compare a halcyon windless summer day with a January gale and gusts that hammer gables and send roof slates into the next townland; compare the arrival of the mailboat in July with its arrival in January. And then consider the islanders, hardy people who can withstand winter months of lashing wind, torrential rain, battering surf, swirling draw, geographic isolation, as well as summer months of hectic tourist inundation when the bulk of the year's income for many is earned during nine intensive weeks.

North Harbour, when the *Naomh Ciaran* berths of a sunny summer Saturday afternoon, has all the makings of a festival. Cars, tractors, empty trailers line the pier, some facing one way, some the other. Young island children splash about in the shallow water out from St. Kieran's Strand, while the older kids learn lifesaving techniques further out, their swimming master shouting instructions on how to effect a rescue; the young offspring of yachtspeople dart here and there in their dinghies, catching fish, spinning round and round; a local transport ship, the *Dun a Riogh*, unloads twenty tons of sand onto three trailers parked along the edge of the adjacent quay outside the safe harbour. It's not just a time to collect the week's groceries, or the food supplements for the cattle, or a new bathtub, or visiting friends; it's a time to people-watch and to visit with neighbours.

North Harbour ninety years ago . . . (Courtesy of the Lawrence Collection).

. . . and as it is now.

Some islanders are content to enjoy the hullabaloo from the comfort of their "bangers"; others mingle with the crowd, or stand next to a neighbour, who's already standing next to a neighbour, and thus a natural line of islanders forms well back from where they know the *Naomh Ciaran* will berth. As the mailboat docks and unloads, the chaos and the fun begin — if you're not in a hurry, that is.

Two local lads leap to the pier from beside the wheelhouse before the boat has been made fast. Once the ropes have been looped over the bollards, pulled taut from the ship, and cleated, a mate unbolts the starboard stern deck door, swings it open, secures it, and out file the hodgepodge of passengers, up the concrete steps, into the mass of vehicles (usually one or two idling, since the salt in the penetrating winds, the consequent swift corrosion, and the general damp don't guarantee a quick start). Visitors and islanders alike slowly thread their way off the pier or eventually climb into one of the cars or vans and wait for the traffic jam to untangle.

Out step islanders back from their errands in Skibbereen, the older ones assisted by one of the mates; German youth, half helmeted, wait anxiously to be handed their bikes from off the bow deck; Irish musicians carry their instruments, ready for a session into the wee hours at the Club; English, Scottish and Irish birdwatchers appear, binoculars dangling from around their necks, telescopes, tripods, and luggage hanging from their shoulders. Out step the eager parents of Irish college students; the young set with their tents and sleeping bags wonder where the campsite is; an assortment of people hope An Oige — the Youth Hostel — isn't full up; day-trippers, with their prams and picnic baskets and shiny shoes, emerge from the passenger saloon. Out step people speaking Düütsch, cockney, Brooklynese, and, of course, Irish. It's hard to distinguish islanders on these days, except maybe the

Naomh Ciaran II.

9

farmers, recognisable by their work clothes and their healthy weathered complexions.

Finally, a large "box" — one of two small ferry containers for supplies, with a volume of 10 cubic meters for the closed box and half that for the open — is lifted by the mailboat's hydraulic hoist and lowered to the pier. The closed box is unlatched, and the friendly ferreting begins. The process has a ritual quality and can't be hurried. Since people are never quite certain how many cartons their telephone-ordered goods will be packed into, they have to examine the label on every box; and thus they can't leave until the last message has been claimed. Consequently, everyone awaiting supplies figuratively, and often literally, bumps into everyone else, greetings and banter flying.

Perhaps because so many people have similar Christian and surnames, but more because there's so much stacking and re-stacking of cardboard boxes, with grown-ups and children carrying other people's supplies to help out, cartons do, albeit rarely, end up in the wrong homes, and further shuffling for a box gone missing ensues, even from one end of the island to the other.

The boat came in at 3:00. The crowd was dispersed by 4:20.

If, however, you wish to see the rule rather than the exception, it's better not to judge by summer activities: islanders are bustling then, what with students, harvests, tourists, regattas, lifeboat days, visiting friends and relatives. And in the evenings, the pubs are so full, visitors cheek by jowl, that many islanders don't bother to have their weekly chat and pint because there's too much noise and crowding to contend with. Far different to observe the Cape off season.

Watch the mailboat come in some Wednesday in mid-January — assuming there's no Force 10 blowing, no heavy draw in the harbour which could render the mailboat as good as rudderless in fast-moving water, and force it to return to Baltimore. A dozen natives along the pier climb in and out of each other's cars to have a chat and keep warm and dry. Periodically they scan the sea for the first sign of the boat's antenna. Instead of docking in the outer harbour, the boat is deftly manoeuvred into the inner, where it's made secure with hawsers six inches in diameter, ropes so heavy when waterlogged that the hydraulic hoist has to be used to lift them into place. Since there are no stone stairs built into the side of the pier, the mate and a bystander wrestle an aluminum railed gangway into position. It balances on the edge for a moment, like a teeter-totter, and then the men on the pier lower it to someone in the stern who guides it into place.

Four local lads disembark. They've had a relaxed long chat during the crossing. One had his hair cut while he was out. Because of the forecast, the trawlers on which two work won't be sailing, so they've come home.

Up the gangway walks an intrepid birdwatcher and a professor from the University of Cork in for his monthly monitoring of the fish farm (a monitoring now done by post). Everyone's well bundled up, and a few wear oilskins. Two middle-aged women emerge. An island couple who had spent a week in Dublin are back from their holidays. An elderly woman in kerchief is handed up the gangway, since it's both steep and slippery and you need to gain careful purchase from the widely-spaced wooden cross-pieces. Then those waiting descend and return from the hold with a dozen cartons of food, some building supplies, a hundredweight bag of supplement cattlefeed. The gangway's pulled up onto the pier, tied securely to a ring. The mate lowers the locking levers over the doors to the hold, the captain locks the wheelhouse, checks the moorings one last time.

At 3:15 the boat came in, at 3:35 the pier was empty. At 10:30 that night seven islanders sit at the bar or on either side of the fireplace in Cotter's Bar and discuss the wind, then the latest oil spill off some foreign coast. Perhaps at 4:00 a.m. the next morning, weather permitting, the captain will move the boat into the outer harbour so that at 9:00 it's not aground at low tide.

Who are these people who seem to thrive on hardship? Are they, as a local historian from Clonakilty told me, "a breed apart"?

I have often wondered whether his comment is germane, though certain that it once was. And I have heard it echoed in various guises throughout mainland villages in West Cork. Indeed, some mainlanders, when they hear I live permanently on Cape, respond, "Aren't they the fierce independent ones?" Or, negatively, "I wouldn't like to be tangling with the likes of 'em." But these are characterisations from afar. When questioned further, most of these people admit to never having visited Cape .

Since Cape has utterly devoted visitors, visitors who come back year after year, decade after decade, I have regularly asked them over a pint or on a birdwalk or while waiting for the mailboat to come in, "What's special about Cape, about Cape islanders?" They generally link the place with the people. Here's a composite answer: "There's no more peaceful, beautiful place, no friendlier people. They have time for you, they get to know you. You walk along their roads and lanes, and when you say hello, they don't just say hello back and continue on their way, they stop and talk; they're genuinely interested in you, they

Cape Clear Regatta Day.

remember you. I know most of the islanders by name, and they know me, and I'm here just a few days a year."

"But isn't that true throughout rural Ireland?" I ask.

"No, not as much so. It's harder to trust people because so many have become so mercenary".

"Even in the country?" I ask, just to be sure.

"Even in the country."

"Well then," I say, "why are Cape islanders special?"

And I receive answers like this: "Cape has kept itself free, free of development. It hasn't the high-speed of modern life. Here you've no two-way roads, rarely can a car get out of second gear; you've no supermarkets, no department stores, no immediate access to essential services, few of the mainland's modern stresses. All you've got is each other. And you all know each other. There's something basically decent about the people here, they have such a sense of humour, they seem highly intelligent, they reflect on things. The older people have a wisdom, and the younger people appear energetic and resolute. I find I can relax here the way I can nowhere else. The air's fresh, the people fresh, and that all helps to recharge my batteries."

As I come to know the islanders better myself, I discover that they are a strong self-reliant people, a proud people, hardworking survivors. The worst thing I could do would be to talk about them individually, for that would turn me into a spy instead of a neighbour and turn them into objects instead of private citizens; it would be like gossiping. So I will limit myself to generalisations; when I do present an individual, he or she is a composite.

I find considerable truth in the description "breed apart". First, most people on the island are O'Driscolls or related to the O'Driscolls. Almost all families — except a few of the blow-ins like mine — are related by blood. Many's the kitchen conversation I've been unable to follow once fourth and fifth cousins begin to be mentioned, or when I discover that some people are related to others through both parents. While infusions of new blood arrive regularly from outside, from other islands, from Dublin, Galway, Kerry, Cork, the O'Driscoll clan dominates the area, including neighbouring Sherkin Island and Baltimore .

Dr Smith, in the 18th Century, wrote of the inhabitants of Cape: they "are generally a very simple honest people, thieving being a vice little known among them ... Most ... are strong and healthy, and are seldom invaded with disorders, dying generally of old age, chiefly owing to their temperate living, hard labour, and clearness of the air."

Trawkieran on a summer's day.

In Lewis's 1837 *Topographical Dictionary*, from which the epigraph to this chapter was taken, we learn that "the island was formerly remarkable for a race of men of extraordinary stature and strength, whose feats are the subject of many interesting narratives." And Donovan, in 1876, wrote: "The natives of Cape Clear are distinct in a great measure from the inhabitants of the mainland; they have remained from time immemorial as a separate colony, always intermarrying amongst themselves; so that we must regard them as amongst the most typical specimens at the present day of the old Milesian race. The name of nearly all the islanders is O'Driscoll or Cadogan, the latter being only a sobriquet for the former ... There can be no doubt but that they were the aboriginal race residing along the sea-coast of Carbery. The isolated position of the island, and its difficulty of approach, have kept its population in a comparatively antique state and distinct condition during the lapse of centuries, so far as nationality and descent. Irish is still the language spoken by nearly all. In features and complexion they bear a strong resemblance to the Spanish race in the Basque provinces and Galicia in the north of Spain, from which provinces, their progenitors migrated to Carbery, and with which country they always preserved a close communication down to the 17th century.

"Until the year 1710 Cape was a sort of established monarchy, an 'imperium in Imperio', and an O'Driscoll — the head of the clan — was always styled 'King of the Island'. They had a code of laws handed down by tradition from father to son, and as strictly obeyed and rigorously administered as if they had been drawn by a Solon or Justinian ... The general punishment was by fine, unless some grave offense was committed, and then the delinquent was banished for ever to the mainland, which was looked upon as a sentence worse even than death.

"The climate is remarkably healthy, none more so in the world, as evidenced by the longevity of the inhabitants, their stalwart frames, healthy appearance, trivial mortality, and freedom from disease. They are a quiet, peaceable, and industrious people, and possess greater gravity of manner, more ponderous bodies, and are built in a larger mould than the more vivacious and excitable race residing on the mainland."

The most frequently cited inherited characteristic has been that of size. Perhaps the most famous man ever to live on Cape was Conchobhar O'Careavaun. He is reputed, writes Burke in 1908, to have been "eight feet high, stout in proportion, and of incredible strength. 'As strong as Crohoor O'Carevaun', is a prevalent saying in

West Cork."

A story still told by islanders runs this way: In Cork Harbour, a group of men were standing on a quay trying to pull toward them a huge anchor some yards out. They hadn't yet been able to budge it. Conchobhar O'Careavaun came walking along, saw the predicament, and asked for a go alone. They stepped aside, seeing the size of him but knowing that no one man could lift what five strong men couldn't. To their amazement, Conchobhar easily raised the anchor. Irritated that what might have been half a day's paid work for them was completed in a matter of minutes, the men mocked Conchobhar, who promptly hefted the anchor, threw it out into the harbour, twice as far as it had been in the first place, and stalked off.

Another story about Conchobhar, told by Donovan and still current, concerns his last days. Perhaps a year before his death, he retired to the Castle of Gold, already a ruin. He roughed it there, living like a hermit, the seas crashing around him, until he died. For many years his shinbone, as if a relic, was exhibited to strangers.

While Donovan adds that "many of the natives, even at present, by their large stature and great strength of body, uphold the credit and tradition of their ancestors such as we never witness in this degenerate age," I'm afraid that one can no longer agree with him. As recently as the nineteen sixties, it was not unusual to drop in to Burke's Pub and see, seated on the bench with their backs against the wall, a group of local men all over six feet. But not today. The island has more than its fair share of tall men, but not so tall that as a group they attract special notice.

What "breed apart" is left on Cape is effected by the island's geography and traditions rather than by its genes. To make it on Cape you have to learn, basically, to do things for yourself; you have to develop self-reliance and hardihood. Mainlanders have a population of tens of thousands to call upon for immediate help, and thus have access to all the specialists that such a population supports. But on Cape, with its tiny population cut off completely from the immediately accessible services most people take for granted, islanders learn not only to do a vast variety of things for themselves, but, more significantly, they develop a mentality, indeed a psychology, that confirms in them that they can *in fact* do most things. Here, I suggest, is what makes the islander a "breed apart".

Back in the sixties, for example, the first automobiles arrived on Cape. While many islanders didn't know how to drive, let alone how to maintain a car, within a year most island men could strip down and reassemble any Beetle engine as well as a trained mechanic could.

Necessity may be the mother of Invention, but she has other children too, "Survival" and "Balin' Wire". One day, for example, the washer in a critical waterline in my house suddenly gave up the ghost; undismayed, my neighbour calmly borrowed my penknife and shaped from the top of his welly the requisite replacement.

Islanders have learned to make a variety of decisions that mainlanders never face, never imagine. Each family has to establish and manage its own dump, since there's no municipal garbage collection. Each family has to determine where its children will attend boarding school after the age of twelve, since the island population cannot support its own secondary school. To go shopping requires considerable organization, and can't be done on the spur of the moment: the mailboat leaves the island, normally, at 9:00 a.m., and for most of the year — the off-season year — it returns at 2:15, tides and weather permitting. If you're in the middle of baling hay, or using the washing machine, or any of a thousand tasks, and a specialised part snaps (and so many parts today are specialised), you normally can't find or purchase a replacement on Cape, and you may well have to wait several days before one can be shipped in, as I had thought would be the case with that washer. The simplest five-minute task, consequently, can sometimes take days if not weeks, and one has to develop a healthy natural philosophy to handle the frustration. Many islanders develop an attitude that enables them both to accept what would drive most contemporary mainlanders to distraction and to get on with the task at hand even when Murphy's law strikes for the *nth* time.

A person from Cape (pejoratively called a Caper), then, learns to depend on himself, herself. When there's some kind of an emergency, an islander's first impulse isn't to reach for the phone to call the hardware store or the electrical appliance shop or the tractor dealer, or any of the multitude of specialists technology has created, but to sit down and figure out how to effect a resourceful solution. Thus, I suggest, people from Cape keep using their common sense and intelligence — usage which might just hone those attributes and bring about what one of Cape's regular visitors, earlier quoted in this chapter, referred to as "wisdom" — instead of relying on someone else's. Yes, islanders are, perforce, a "breed apart": They don't simply survive the stark seasonal contrasts, the weather, the geographic isolation — they thrive on them.

Chapter Three
The Passage Tomb

*… a humped whale-shaped island whose people remain Irish speaking
and have always contained themselves and their secrets beyond
Ireland.*

Peter Somerville-Large's *The Grand Irish Tour*

Passage tomb art motifs — three spirals, chevrons, circumscribing zigzags — on the justly famous Cape Clear Stone gave birth to the belief that a passage tomb erected in pre-historic times should be somewhere on the southernmost of Irish islands. On June 20th and 21st, 1993, Paddy O'Leary, West Cork archaeologist, made a discovery that has both national and international implications, and which logically locates where the stone was originally erected perhaps five millennia back.

The peregrinations of the Neolithic stone, now housed in the Cork Public Museum in Fitzgerald Park, deserve detailed telling, for they start the trail to discovery.

In 1874, in a long narrow field that constituted part of Tom Shipsey's farm in the island townland of Croha West, Dónal O Síocháin and Conchúr O Ríogáin, while clearing the field, found the stone. Shards of old incised pottery were spotted in the area as well, but they "grew legs" overnight.

Farmer Shipsey sent the stone to the Reverend John O'Leary, CC, who had once lived on Cape but had moved to nearby Sherkin Island. The good Father planted the decorated stone in his garden, and there it stayed. On his elevation to parish priest of Clonakilty, Father O'Leary left Sherkin. The stone lay there until re-discovered in 1945 and sent to University College, Cork. The late Professor M.J. O'Kelly wrote a note in the *Journal of the Cork Historical and Archaeological Society* in 1949; he suggested that the presence of the stone on Cape Clear led him to assume that "Passage-grave folk" had erected a tomb on the island.

In 1984 Eammon Lankford, curator of the new Cape Heritage Centre, wrote to the director of the Cork County survey and asked him to survey Cape. That April four archaeologists visited Cape from a Monday through to Friday. Paired up, one group discovered that St. Kieran's pillar stone had, in addition to the two incised crosses, a panel on its southeastern side, within the borders of which faint Celtic interlacings could be detected. It appeared that this pagan art was dressed out of the stone when it was christianised.

Atop Cnoc Caraintín (Quarantine Hill), the island's highest point at 533 feet, the second pair discovered the ruins of a prehistoric tomb. The ruins consist of a sub-circular spread of boulders and smaller stones, and measure 16.5m northeast by southwest, and 14m northwest by southeast. In the centre lies a small chamber, lined on three sides by orthostats (vertical slabs) and open toward the northeast. A line of 5 small orthostats also pointing toward the northeast occurs between the chamber and the perimeter of the circle and may represent one side of the passage entrance to the chamber. With stones from the ruins, a dry-stone pillar to the northwest of the chamber was probably erected in the 1840's by the Ordnance Surveyors as a tri-angulation point. Once the circular area was probably heaped high in a mound of stones, now collapsed and partly pilfered.

In the 1989 *Journal of the Cork Historical and Archaeological Society*, Paddy O'Leary published an article entitled "A Passage Tomb on Clear Island in West Cork?" To substantiate his proposal that the site is probably a passage tomb, he notes that the decorated stone was found only half a mile away, that the circular tomb is built on the island's highest hilltop, that a chamber was found which faces in the

Archaeologist Paddy O'Leary (4th from left) and group form a "stone circle".

same direction as a line of stones which probably mark the line of passage, that the orientation is northeastern. All these facts point to the passage tomb explanation.

When I telephoned Paddy in July of 1993 to confirm that the tomb was orientated on the summer solstice sunrise, he provided me first with the history of his involvement with the site since 1984. He, it turned out, was one of the four who conducted the survey that year, a time which marked the beginning of his love affair with the site. With fellow archaeologist Lee Snodgrass he continued to visit the tomb until they were reasonably satisfied that the orientation was on the summer solstice sunrise. They then had the Archaeology Section of the Ordnance Survey complete an instrument survey. His 1989 article followed. On the night before the summer solstice in 1992, he slept at Cnoc Caraintín to see what happened at sunrise, but cloud cover obscured the sun.

On June 20th, 1993, Paddy was ready and waiting. And, like celestial clockwork, at last, there it was, in a cloudless golden dawn: on the horizon 5 miles NNW of Rosscarbery, in the gap formed by Carrigfadda (Long Rock), which reaches to 1031', and the next hill to the north, Carrigagrenane, which rises to 900'; there, in the valley between the two hills, in line with the passage and shining into the chamber, rose the solstice sun, manifesting itself in the lowest point of the gap. Twenty-two miles from Cnoc Caraintín, the gap perfectly framed the emergent disk.

Unlike Newgrange with its roof box and winter solstice orientation, Cape Clear joins Cairn U at Lough-Crew, Co. Meath, and Sess Kilgreen, Co. Tyrone, as having an authenticated summer solstice alignment.

Perhaps we'll never know how many centuries of cultural accretion went into the building of these tombs, but at least one question has recently been answered: Paddy's nine year's of detective work confirm that Cape has a passage tomb with a solar orientation. And they confirm that the Cape Clear Stone hails not from Croha West but from Cnoc Caraintín.

In a letter to me, Paddy further elaborated on the meaning of his finding: "The discovery of the tomb and of an orientation on the

Cape Clear Stone.

Summer Solstice rising sun is of great importance. It is important nationally in that it is the first authenticated passage tomb in County Cork; it is important internationally because it further re-inforces the growing belief that all our passage tombs do have astronomical orientations. When we realize that Newgrange passage tomb is the oldest astronomically orientated structure in the world, and that passage tombs in Ireland are generally regarded as falling within the mid-Neolithic period (c. 3,000 BC), we can see the evidence of widespread knowledge of astronomy in pre-historic Ireland at a very early date.

"This interest in astronomy continues through the Bronze Age in stone circles, stone rows and tombs. An excavation at the Cape Clear passage tomb would be of great assistance in helping us to compare dates with the great tombs of the Boyne Valley. There has been, for years, debate as to whether those great tombs come at the beginning or the end of the passage tomb sequence of building in Ireland. This might be an opportunity to decide the issue."

Next, in August 1993, I joined a tour of lay archaeologists Paddy brought to Cape and shared with him some sites I had found that are in alignment with the tomb, and then we visited Cape's most famous standing stones, which include "The Marriage Stone" with its rare

10 minutes after sunrise on 20 June, 1993. (Courtesy Paddy O'Leary).

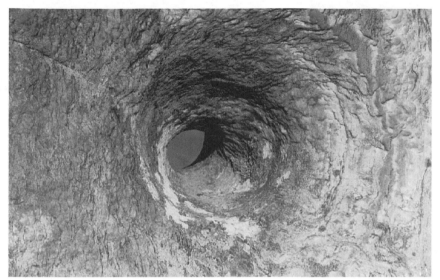

"I pledge my troth."

hole, through which, allegedly, people have pledged their troth down through the millennia. We discovered that the axis of the hole points toward the very spot where the summer solstice sun rises. We also discovered that if we fourteen formed a circle keeping the same distance between each member as the two standing stones have, and which repeated the angle the two stones have to each other, that our "standing stone and standing people" circle had a diameter of about nine meters. Initially sceptical of a stone circle having been here before, Paddy could no longer dismiss the possibility.

With a "boulder burial" not more than a few dozen stone throws away, with an alleged Neolithic cooking place (*fulacht fiadh* or *fulacht fiann*, the cooking place of deer or in a wilderness), other standing stones and probable graves in the vicinity, and the passage tomb quietly above us, we could but delightedly wonder about the significant Neolithic population sea-girt Cape must once have supported.

Paddy's indefatigable, careful scholarship quietly and modestly raises a question irresistible to the journalist in me: Are Cape's picturesque site and modest tomb earlier or contemporary with "earliest" Newgrange? And as I speculate on what a team of trained archaeologists may discover in this area, I come to realize that we could do worse in this world than spend time and energy, as the ancients did, to orient ourselves properly. Perhaps passage tombs are but stony metaphors meant to remind us of heavenly directions.

Glen West Wall.

Eclipsed

In bed, out of a dead sleep, I vaguely heard
the morning news, reference to car-bombs and eclipse.
That night, on my devious way back to bed,
which in fair weather takes me outside
for a final reconnoitering, I beheld the silver
arrogance of mistress moon at the full; I checked
her dazzling sea for passing ships, across her harbour
for lights, and up our shimmering Glen.

Albeit she cast uncanny light over all the usual,
I hit the hay, satisfied, ker-plunk.
Only then did I recall mention of eclipse.
Absently I lifted the curtains at the head of the bed.
No, she showed no sign of any celestial tampering.
Relieved I'd missed nothing, I rolled over,
acquiescing, may have heard my wife put out the light,
and woke to morning fog.

Then I learned stark fact: the likes of that eclipse
— which my wife had watched from 7 minutes after eleven until
almost one — a total lunar eclipse of a full moon,
would not occur again for ninety-two years.
Hmmm.

A tough-nut friend whispers from some back chamber of my

                                                        mind:

A mistake once made's a mistake forever. Well, dummy,
what's to do but try to miss a little less tomorrow.

Chapter Four
The Castle of Gold

From the vicinity of Dunanore, we obtain a view of the coast and the surrounding ocean, which is one of surpassing beauty, when the summer sun is setting in the far west.

Daniel Donovan's *Sketches in Carbery*

Pirates, impregnable island fortress, castle, cannonballs, hidden treasure, fairies; all these romantic and connotative words associate themselves with an ancient structure silhouetted against sea and sheer high cliffs, with the Fastnet Lighthouse often visible four miles beyond. This O'Driscoll Castle claims considerable history, legend, fireside tale. As one of the most salient ruins of Cape, Dunanore — the Castle of Gold — deserves special exploration, literary, photographic and physical.

After viewing the castle on a multitude of cliff walks, and hearing stories not only about what had there transpired but about the dangers of visiting it, I began to wonder what comment Dunanore has provoked through the centuries. In my quest, I was able to trace relevant written history back as far as Charles Smith, who visited Cape in 1770, and who described part of his visit this way: "There is a very narrow passage, about a yard broad and ten yards in length, to this castle. The path is high and steep on both sides, the sea on either side being so deep, that few persons well used to it will venture to walk it over. When I got to the top of the castle, and saw the ocean rolling on all sides of the rock, I wished heartily to be on the mainland again."

Still searching, I made my circuitous way to the Zurich Central Library. There I happened upon a rare 17th century map of Munster (with Cape showing itself as wooded), by a Dutch cartographer, as well as the 1837 encyclopedic reference work, Samuel Lewis's *Topographical Dictionary of Ireland*, in which, under the Cape Clear Island section, this sentence whet my appetite: "At the south-west

The Castle of Gold at Sunset.

point of the island, overhanging the sea, and accessible only by a narrow and dangerous pathway, not more than three feet in breadth, are the ruins of Dunanore castle, or the 'Golden Fort', which, from its distance from all landing places, would appear to have been built more for the purpose of a safe retreat in case of invasion, than for defence of the shores: the view from the battlements is very extensive, and embraces a great variety of objects of a bold and imposing character."

An islander, a ship captain born in 1900, on seeing my enthusiasm on matters Cape, loaned me his first edition copy of *Sketches in Carbery* (1876), in which Donovan noticed certain changes: "A short distance to the west of Tra-Kieran, on a projecting rocky headland ... we observe the ruins of Dunanore Castle .... By the continual action of the waves the narrow passage has been nearly washed away, and the height above the water level is only a few feet; in fact, sometimes at high water the castle plateau becomes completely insulated."

Returning to the 20th century, I bought a copy of Sommerville-Large's *The Coast of West Cork*, 1972. He too wrote on our theme: "The Golden Fort is perhaps the most dramatically sited of the O'Driscoll castles, set among cliffs and sea birds on what is virtually a small island. At one time a narrow causeway linked it to the mainland; now it can just be reached by a hazardous climb over tumbled rocks.

Built in the thirteenth century, it was a typical three-storyed structure placed in a seemingly impregnable look-out position over the bay and the mainland."

The last book-mention I could find occurs in the unfortunately out-of-print *Natural History of Cape Clear*, 1974. One contributor to this ornithological delight, S.L.C. Fogden, wrote of the area where the castle is located: "This stretch of the shoreline is one of the most spectacular on the island. Standing above the strategically placed O'Driscoll Castle one can look right along the ragged coast to Trawleagaigh and across the five miles of Roaringwater Bay to Mount Gabriel standing above Schull and the ranges of mountains beyond. Seen with the right light highlighting the sea, white on starkly outlined rocks, there is no more dramatic scenery anywhere."

Why should one tiny ruin of a castle receive such attention? My interest fully piqued, in the summer of 1992, with my athletic daughter and even more athletic future son-in-law for security and companionship, with permission from the owner of the land on which the castle is situated, with awareness of that day's tides so that they wouldn't cut us off, and with a coil of rope knotted every three feet for hand-grips, I set out to visit the castle rather than merely to view it from the island proper, for the narrow causeway referred to above no longer exists. Carefully looping one end of the rope to a stone in a nearby fence, hand over hand lowering ourselves one after another down the almost vertical twenty feet to the small strand below, and quickly scrambling up the incline to the castle, we suddenly found ourselves powerfully excited, as though we had just climbed a formidable peak. My heart was pounding not so much from exertion and danger but from excitement and delight at finally being able to examine this monument close-up.

While nothing more than a ruined minor stronghold, the Castle of Gold suddenly acquired dimensions that it didn't have when observed from Cape proper. We spent an afternoon there, climbing the stairs, exploring the basement rooms, marvelling at the massive archways, gazing at the sea through the remaining windows, mostly imagining what it must have been like some 600 years ago.

Now it makes more sense when I read Donovan's periodic prose: "Dunanore (the Golden Fort) is supposed to have been first erected about the beginning of the 13th century; the ruins at present consist of a portion of the side walls of the central tower or donjon, the eastern wall has fallen to the ground, but so firmly united together are the stones, by the grouting process used in the masonry, that the greater part of the fallen structure remains in one solid mass. Nearly all traces of the outer building which surrounded the tower, viz., bastions, curtains, &c., and the dwellings which were occupied by the chieftain's retainers, have disappeared .... The chambers overhanging the stormy Atlantic are tenantless and deserted, except by the birds of the air; the ancient tapestry and the ornaments which decked the walls are replaced by a luxuriant covering of the ivy green; and the only music now which re-echoes round this crumbling pile is the mournful wail of the winter wind, the sighing of the summer breeze, and the constant cadence of the Atlantic roar."

Donovan goes on in this vein, finally confessing, so enraptured of the beauty from this spot is he , that "no pen can properly describe nor pencil delineate, nor painter's skill portray: dissolving views and transformation scenes ...."

The castle, and the fortunes of Sir Fineen O'Driscoll (from whose family most of the islanders are descended), came to an end on 22 March, 1601. Captain Roger Harvey captured Cape and the castle, having mounted his cannons on high ground above the promontory, and blasted away. Now only these ruins and the stories remain. Here's a version, patched together and embroidered, of two of the tales:

Once upon a time, in the reign of Queen Anne, when a garrison of red-coated British soldiers was stationed on Cape, a young sergeant, far from home, far from his girl, heard stories about a mysterious ship which, with snow-white sails, anchored just off the Castle of Gold. The ship came always at midnight. And then, right after midnight, a ghostly crew unloaded a cargo of golden ingots and coins, which the

Dunanore in Winter.

26

men lugged up to the castle and buried below the eastern wall. Many's the time that mysterious ship and that ghostly crew have been seen and heard, the men singing and carousing through the night. But when dawn comes, the phantom ship and its phantom crew vanish like mist in a sudden wind, and not a crumb nor a golden coin has ever been found in the light of day.

Hearing this story, the sergeant thought more and more about the treasure, and finally determined to unearth it. Surely, he thought, a castle couldn't be called the Castle of Gold unless there was some truth to the name; surely the tale of the ghostly ship had some bit of truth behind it; surely some treasure is buried beneath the walls of Dunanore. And why shouldn't I be the one to find it?

Whenever the moon was so full and the sky so clear that he could see his shadow of a summer or autumn night, he'd steal off to Dunanore to dig. Now and then while digging he'd spring to attention, having heard the splash of an oar, the luff of a sail, the laugh of a man. But each time the sea showed herself serenely empty, as if mocking him, and he'd return to his work. He dug and dug, creating a pit six feet square, and three, six, ten feet deep, but still no gold. At last he reached the level of the sea. When he had found nothing but sand and shells of the sea, he gave up and, I assure you, he never dug another hole his entire life long. I also assure you that the treasure remains well hidden.

Indeed, the last time I viewed the castle what should I observe but a large black tug standing off from the towering cliffs. As I watched, I saw a Zodiac leave the mother ship and make a number of mysterious rendezvous in the nearby waters. Finally, I discerned that the outboard was servicing scattered pairs of deep-sea divers. The search for the treasure of Dunanore goes on from century to century.

Chapter Five
Shipwreck

… certain coasts are set apart for shipwreck.

Robert Louis Stevenson

C ape has often proven a welcome port in storm, and many's the ship that has gratefully stood in to North or South Harbour. But the island's exposed position, her formidable cliffs, the infamous Gascanane cross-currents and frequent tidal race, Roaring Water Bay and its submerged rocks, pea-soup fogs, swells that break for the first time in thousands of miles, all make Cape's jagged coast a veritable graveyard of ships. So before you "come in" for today's excursion, may I suggest that first you visit Bushe's Pub in Baltimore. Regular visitors, residents and captain and crew of the *Naomh Ciaran* congregate daily here for a pot of tea, a pint, a bowl of soup, a fresh salmon sandwich, a chat. This establishment, as much museum as pub, has on every inch of wall maritime artifacts: brass fittings, antique barometers, signal lanterns, photographs of the lifeboat at the Fastnet, models of tall ships — and scattered amidst all the relics and wreckage hang various navigational charts, one of which shows the location of shipwrecks, which ring Cape round.

Now that you are well fortified and oriented, have made the crossing to Cape, and have had a leisurely stroll from North Harbour to the wharf at South Harbour, climb aboard this one-time island fishing boat, the *Golden Seeker*, which I have commandeered for the day, and join me for a clockwise circumnavigation of Cape. An islander's at the helm, and be assured that throughout the history of the south coast, Cape islanders have been known as the best pilots of all. He's my guide, I'll be yours. I'll point out the sites of various wrecks; maybe one day you'll arrive on the tugboat *Cabot*, or on one of the small fishing boats for hire, and do some underwater detective work of your own at one of the locations I'll be showing you.

Before we cast off, note the substantial iron loop fixture imbedded on the wharf. And over there, on the beach, near where a new stretch of seawall was constructed in the fall of 1992, you can spot what's left of an iron mast. They're the only remaining evidence of an event that took place during World War II. In January of 1940 the coaster *SS Maigue* beached in South Harbour in front of the priest's house, the captain having mistaken the priest's lights for those of Baltimore. Liam Ó Loideoin, in his *Walker's Guide to Cape Clear Island,* tells the rest of the story: "The priest roused the islanders to render assistance and for his help was rewarded with a leg of bacon, part of the ship's cargo. For many years, the islanders teased the good Father by suggesting that he had wrecked the steamship for a leg of bacon. The ship was refloated using a system of winches and tackles and with the help of 30 men."

Cast off bow and stern ropes! Haul in the fenders! Please note that life jackets are stowed under the board benches where you're seated. We've two hours of fairly slack tide, a neap tide at that, the sea's a millpond, the glass at 1020 and rising.

See how the harbour is like two harbours, an inner and an outer? There, to the west, before the inner harbour widens into the outer, you spot a series of small caves with step-like rocks leading down to them; that's where the Spanish used to sell contraband to the islanders. And now that we're into the outer harbour, the little cove you see to starboard is called *Coosa-galloony*, and may well be named as a consequence of the oldest shipwreck for which I have found any record. A Spanish galleon ran aground here in about 1620. Legend has it that the ship was seeking shelter, and, with sails furled, came to her end in that vicinity. I've watched a thirty foot basking shark ply those very waters.

Yes, now that we're out of the harbour, you do feel significantly more movement, the lazy steady swells coming from the west. But not to

The South Coast.

29

The Old Telegraph House and The Asgard.

worry. We'll keep well out from the cliffs where the waters churn on even this most halcyon of days.

Between the Blananarragaun, the formidable long western point of South Harbour and a favorite haunt of intrepid birdwatchers intent on seabird passage, and Foilnalunga (half a mile to the northwest), you observe Cape's southernmost stretch. Somewhere along here the *SS Nestorian* was sunk in 1916; she was carrying steel and shellheads from New York to Liverpool. For the last few summers a group of divers vacationing in the area have been bringing up ingots from this wreck. One salvager told me that they pay for their vacation with their discoveries, but he became tightlipped when he saw my curiosity remain unabated.

This long point is called the Bill of Clear, or *Pointanardatruha*. It's Cape's most westerly headland. In 1934 the *Trial* was abandoned by her crew near the Mizen Head; she then drifted to Cape and sank off the Bill, her cargo of timber salvaged before she sank. By the way, note all the kittiwakes resting on the Bill's protected ledges. Have you ever wondered why they have such black legs?

There's Dunanore coming into view. During World War II, a Spanish trawler — fishing without lights — floundered on the rocks by the castle; her sister ship, following immediately behind her, met the same fate. I've watched divers scouring the bottom of Coosadoona — the cove between the castle and the island — for treasure.

To the north, to port, we can now make out the West, Middle, and East Calf Islands. Although she wrecked on the nearby West Calf Island rather than Cape, mention should be made of the *Stephen Whitney*, which went down in 1847 with one hundred lives lost. This disaster dramatised the inadequacy — the poor location — of Cape's lighthouse. As a newspaper of that time wrote: "The deciding factor in terminating Clear Island Lighthouse was perhaps the loss of the *Stephen Whitney*, an American packet ship, which had taken twenty-two days to cross the Atlantic, the final two or three days, according to survivors, was in dense fog .... The Skipper apparently mistook Crookhaven lighthouse for Old Head before heading out to sea and eventually being wrecked."

In January of 1909, in a savage gale, the *Savona* went down, either on Cape or one of the Calves, it was never known for certain. Regardless, *The Cork Examiner* reported that along Cape's western cliffs "quantities of wreckage have been floating about ... (the rescuing) tug masters and crew who could not find the ship and who braved the elements so doggedly deserved a better reward for their action, but the sea in its fury deprived them of a valuable prize."

This northern side of Cape is its most protected area, its leeward side, so to speak, and hence has had few wrecks. That's Bird Island, *Illauneana*, that long raised ridge — and those dozens of silhouetted vulturish birds are shags. There's one in a classic pose, drying its wings by holding them motionlessly outstretched. When the *Naomh Ciaran* comes in to Cape through the "southern" route past the Baltimore Beacon, or Lot's Wife, it threads its way through this narrow channel between Bird and Cape, thrilling tourists. Locals tell the story that in the days of the O'Driscoll pirates, the pirates, when given chase, would duck back into these waters, shoot through this narrow channel, knowing where the rocks were, and delight to see their pursuers founder.

Hang on. We're passing through the infamous, roiling Gascanane Sound, one of the most dangerous stretches of water on the southwest coast. This region kicks up viciously heightened waves, especially when the tidal current flows against the swells, the wind, or both. Add to them the fast flow of a spring tide, and you've a witch's boiling cauldron. Whew, since canoeing across here once in a southerly, I'm always thankful to be safely through. There used to be a tradition that someone new to Cape composed a verse while crossing the Gascanane for the first time. The verse propitiated the spirit of the place. Perhaps O'Donovan Rossa's Irish lines (in an English translation) are the most famous:

> Oh white-breasted Gascanane, you of the angry current,
> Let me and all with me pass you in safety;
> Stay calm, my secret beloved, and do not drown me,
> And I give my word that to Cape I shall never return.

Off the port side you can see Kedge Island. There's a sizeable channel that runs straight through it, though we can't see it from this angle. To starboard you see that we're again running parallel to Cape's savagely exposed land. Recently I saw pleasure divers prowling this swirling bottom for half days at a go, but I failed to make contact with them, nor did I ever see them bring anything up. Yet something held their interest.

Having passed around Cape's eastern end, we're heading southwest. Since this area borders the main sea route in to the fully protected waters between Sherkin Island and Baltimore, many is the ship that has passed these dangerous shores in hopes of shortly finding refuge from a gale or hurricane. Sobering it is to recall headlines in *The Cork Examiner* on April 26th, 1894, which proclaimed: "THE STORM",

"Appalling Loss of Life and Property", "Nine Fisherman Drowned Near Baltimore", "Boats and Nets Swept Away", "Narrow Escapes and Gallant Rescues". The article itself begins: "It is to be hoped that few places can claim the saddening list of disasters that now makes Baltimore [and thus Cape] conspicuous." This desolate coastline, then, has many sad stories to tell.

Perhaps ironically, many ships have gone down below the Old Lighthouse, which sits atop that massive stone bowl a mile ahead to starboard. In 1955 a French trawler broke up immediately below it. And then there's the story of the *Illyrian*. The report in a local newspaper of that time sounds like an adventure story today. Let me read you the article from May 19th, 1884: "The 'steamship' *Illyrian*, of the Leyland Line, ... ran on the rocks off the Old Lighthouse, Cape Clear, on Thursday night, and has become a total wreck .... The ill-fated vessel left Liverpool for Boston with a large cargo on Wednesday afternoon, and all went well until the evening of Thursday, when a dense fog set in. The speed of the vessel was reduced to seven knots and the fog whistle was kept going at frequent intervals, and soundings were repeatedly taken. Captain Farquharson ... was under the impression that Cape Clear had been passed, but as the fog still prevailed the speed of the vessel was not increased, and as there was no apprehension of danger, one watch retired tó their bunks. It was exactly twenty-five minutes past eleven o'clock on Thursday night when the steamer ran on the rocks with great force, causing the greatest excitement amongst the crew and passengers — the sailors describe the latter as 'cattle men' — but the excitement was soon allayed by the captain and officers of the ship, who acted with great coolness and self-possession. The boats were at once partially lowered, but owing to the darkness and the fact tĥat there was no immediate danger of loss of life, they were not launched until daylight on Friday morning. In the meantime guns were fired, and also signal rockets, but these were neither seen nor heard on shore .... The captain and crew remained by the vessel until she keeled over .... and all on board ... were safely landed in Baltimore.

"The cargo consisted for the most part of wool and brandy and whiskey, and it is expected that a large portion of it will be saved. Many bales of wool and casks of spirits have, however, been washed out of the vessel, and many boats are out all along the coast in the hope of picking up salvage ....

"The crew are in a most destitute condition, having been discharged on Saturday morning, by order of the owners, with only three days' pay to each man. Many of them, too, have lost their clothing .... Some of them left on Saturday evening intent upon walking to Cork, but remained in Skibbereen over Sunday ...."

In 1867 a wreck occurred, though I haven't heard exactly where. The *Cork Advertiser* provided this stark account: "The ship, *Czar*, of Glasgow, was a few days ago found deserted off Cape Clear. She was loaded with iron and coal, and when picked up bore traces of having sustained a severe gale. Not a living creature was on board."

Ah, here's the Bullig. We're back, safe and sound, to South Harbour, a safe port in all but a southerly — but then of no help at all. We've seen but a sprinkling of the wreck sites; I fear that there are many others. I can't be definitive. Islanders speak of settles made with ship timber, of a stairway, of an entire house built from such timber, of various heroic rescues in the middle of the night.

You may have noticed that Cape has its fair share of cemeteries: St. Ciaran's at North Harbour, the Protestant Cemetery behind the Youth Hostel (where the tall trees are swaying in this suddenly freshening breeze), a small graveyard for unbaptised infants in Ballyieragh (straight up that boreen from the Palace, and across the road from that white farmhouse), Killickaforavane at the crossroads, Cill Bhrún in Comillane. But generally unnoticed, along the tops of some of the headlands, are stone markers for unknown drowned sailors, buried above the sea they knew so intimately. In fact, there's a series of such graves on the high ground above the Bullig, which we just passed. Locals tell me that it was traditional to bury unknown drowned s ailors above where they washed ashore.

Like most jagged wind-swept ocean islands, Cape has a sailor and ship graveyard circumscribing it. I speculate that the strange surrounding and pervasive presence of death by shipwreck and disaster adds to the feeling of precious, vibrant life — and acts as midwife at the birth of a *Carpe Diem* philosophy belonging to some Cape islanders. The sea and its amoral acts help to determine even the psychology of those who live beside it, and especially of those who are surrounded by it, of those who live on it. A forgiving fatalism in attitude, a painful final shrug of the shoulders upon news of tragedy, a smile coming through a face of suffering, enable a hardened but sensitive dwindling people to get on with their lives.

That's it, we've safely finished our circumnavigation of Cape. I confess I'm not certain I'd like to know the detail of all treasures we've passed over, for then I'd also likely have to know the exact nature of all tempestuous tragedies played out along our route. What's to do but toss the fenders over, please. The *Golden Seeker*'s back. Careful. Ah well, that's what a rub rail's for.

Chapter Six

Disaster

The central event in the following short story is drawn from newspaper accounts of what happened on Tuesday, November 18th, 1919; the rest is island lore and embroidery. CK

In early morning, while searching for the family sow, young Pat kept his weather eye on what he hoped would prove a keg of brandy. At first he'd thought it nothing but a small clump of flotsam, a knot of tangled kelp, a large loose buoy, but as it kept bobbing there, off to the west, not far from the Fastnet, moving closer and closer to Cape with the incoming tide, he'd set his heart on a keg of brandy.

He'd heard the stories. Back when, his grandfather had often related, back in the middle of the seventeen hundreds, a visitor to Cape, an historian, had spent a week on the island observing the antiquities, the people, their way of life. This man Smith had approved everything he found, the friendliness, the purity of life, the hard working men and women, their honesty and hospitality — except for one characteristic: their random drunkenness, men and women alike. And at all hours, mind you.

How his grandfather had chortled at the description. For what Smith the careful historian hadn't realised was that a recent shipwreck near Carriglure had launched a cargo of oaken brandy barrels — and the islanders had rescued the barrels from a fate worse than death, a wasteful oblivion against the wave-dashed cliffs. To be on the safe side, they had effected a thorough rescue and been sufficiently foresighted so as to hide the barrels about the island — in the opening to a secret well, or underneath a hay cock, or on a ledge above the splash zone within a cave — as a protection against the gombeen men and British soldiers who were sure to investigate the incident.

So when Meg went out to bring in the cattle for their evening

Black skies to the west.

milking, or when Donal went the circuitous route down to the harbour to check on his boat, or when Mary set off to haul fresh water from the well, or when Ciaran trudged through the furze and fern to overlook his cattle, they all had a spot where they secretly stopped and drew a swig, or two, in fact pretty regular nips, so unprecedented was the availability of bountiful brandy. And your man Innocent Smith had arrived on Cape not long after this harvest from the amoral sea — and subsequently pronounced his misguided judgment.

Not since the Spaniards used to "hold court", as Pat's grandfather said, along the rocky, step-like banks of inner South Harbour, and sell their wares, cigars and cognac especially, had the islanders had such unusual pleasure. And around the time of Charles Smith's visit, their imbibing had cost them nary a penny.

Now this early morning in 1919, Pat had climbed the hill behind his house in search of a rambunctious sow that had burrowed her way out of a ramshackle pen. Since she was about to litter, he didn't want her running free, for last time she had shown a propensity to roll her massive bulk over on her farrow; once, she had eaten two of her new-born. Fecund she was, yes, he thought; but outrageously and unintentionally brutal too. So while Pat was herding Deirdre back, with the help of his wire-haired terrier, who nipped at her heels, he had spotted the mesmeric object out to sea, and marked it with great anticipation.

With the pregnant, grunting, belly-swinging Deirdre safely enclosed, and the hole plugged with stone from atop a nearby wall, Pat stomped back to the high knoll and resumed his vigil. He checked the moon, a half moon, and knew that low tide would have been around six. That meant the flood would slack near noon. He decided to put out in his punt at 11:15. Near 11:30 the keg would have been carried about as close to the island as it would come. He was beginning to feel excitement. He imagined having a whole keg of brandy to himself. But he would share it, too, he would, he promised; and sure but the sharing could be as pleasurable as the having.

It was then he spotted the *Roving Swan* heading for Schull. Would his friends John, and Paddy, and Hugh, and that other John, and old Mister Cadogan, would they spot his treasure? With considerable trepidation, he watched them motor toward Schull in their fishing boat, all forty-four feet of her. To his relief, they never deviated from their course, not by a hand's-breadth. They had, after all, several dozen boxes of fish to sell, supplies to purchase.

By 11:15 Pat had unmoored his small skiff, rounded the Bull's Nose, and sallied forth from the mouth of North Harbour. The swells were long and slow, like tier after tier of sunken barren hills. He established a steady rhythm, careful to keep strength in reserve. Once past Ship's Bottom — *Tonelunge* — a seemingly insignificant rock not far from the O'Driscoll Castle, but one before which waves reared up like fierce horses and on which they crashed mountainous even in the flattest of seas, and around which the sea was ever full of alarming cross-currents, Pat began regularly twisting around on his thwart to take a bead on the keg. And then he felt his mouth turn dry: There, to the north, was the *Roving Swan*, returning prematurely from Schull with what old Bernard Cadogan called "domestic requirements". She'd just rounded the westernmost of the three Calves.

While they were two miles off, and about the same from the brandy, and while he was only a quarter of a mile from his treasure, they had a motor. He upped his pace. Then he noted that they had changed their direction, that the rev of their engine had increased. They had clearly spotted both him and the merrily bobbing keg he had set his heart on. By way of a joke, they clearly hoped to thwart his efforts.

He rowed. He rowed now with all reserves cast to the four winds, runnels of sweat soon marking his weathered young face. His eyes began to sting. Every now and then he'd hurriedly crane his neck around to make certain he was on course — and to judge what progress he was making compared to that of the *Roving Swan*. It would be close. It was a race to the almighty finish.

He gritted his teeth and tore into the swells, the thin long oars flying. At the end of every stroke he gave a sudden flick so that the oars seemed first to bow and then to pop out of the sea and splash down well behind him without any discernible loss in the boat's momentum. He no longer bothered to feather the oars. He was flying.

Despite his labour, he grinned, his tongue pressed against the back of his lower front teeth: What was having ten or fifteen squirming piglets compared to having a cask of aromatic brandy? And then he downright laughed, all caution to the winds: What was having a keg of brandy compared to winning this race!

The *Roving Swan* bore down on him. Only a hundred yards to go, he thought; first one there has all the rights. He dug in the blades. The miniature whirlpools his oars left to stern leapt and foamed. He could feel their engine nearing, and above the piercing growl of the motor he could recognize his pals' shouts of glee. With less than forty yards to go they were alongside, they cut in front of him. Their wake hit his punt and he had to turn into it to avoid being capsized. Their victory cheers as they had steamed ahead were hard in his ears. Panting, drenched with sweat and the spray from hitting the wake, he shipped oars and watched the five fishermen prepare to claim what he had coveted, what he had thought his treasure.

Suddenly — as when the torpedo-configured blue shark attacks out

Cliff and sea rescue team, Foilacuslaun.

38

of nowhere — the tone of the playful victory jubilation turned to terror. Hugh and John, who were in the bow, screamed in unison, "Hard to starboard, hard to starboard." And then Pat knew what Hugh and John knew, and then everybody knew.

The sound of the explosion was heard along the mainland coast from the Mizen to Galley Head. It reverberated through the stone foundations of Cape Clear Island. In every island house dressers rattled, cups and saucers broke. In some island houses hunks of plaster dropped off the walls. One nine-year-old girl told Pat later that she had thought the world was coming to an end. Her family's front door slammed shut in the thunderous shock; prized crockery fell about her feet, shattering on the flags.

Pat couldn't believe his eyes. In the reverberating blast the *Roving Swan* disappeared; in its place was a violent momentary geyser — and matchwood, matchwood raining down, a sea gone mad. He saw bodies, or bits of bodies — he wasn't sure in all the chaos — one hundred feet in the air, turning, turning. Had the *Roving Swan* not been between him and the floating horn mine, his punt — and himself in it, the victor — would have been raining down matchwood, and bits and pieces, too.

Above him he watched a body, as if in slow motion, turn and turn. He watched aghast as the body plummeted down, splashed, disappeared. Without knowing what he was doing, he rowed to the centre of the site. Less than a year ago, he recalled, some of these selfsame friends had rescued sailors from the *Hazelside*, a British freighter torpedoed twelve miles off the Fastnet, and from the *Nestorian* as well, and now here he was, perhaps rescuing the rescuers. And Hugh's brother, too — he couldn't prevent the thought from crowding in — had drowned within the year. It's not just the sea but war, Pat thought; war's a terrible time, whether you were in it or not; war has a way of reaching out and murdering anyone handy.

War's a worm of a thing, he found himself thinking; you can't tell head from tail. And while he hadn't yet seen a worm of the sea, he'd heard the old men talk of the worms; and he'd heard that the graybeards before them had talked of worms too, of worms eight feet, ten feet long, longer. You never knew what would appear, what would happen, what would indiscriminately lash out. "The very divil incarnate," he heard himself say aloud in the midst of the solemn hush that had fallen. Inexplicably, he found himself seeing in his mind's eye lazy Deirdre heaving her bulk over onto her own children, squashing them, grunting peaceably.

Abeam, as if bobbing up from another realm, appeared eighty-eight year old Mr. Cadogan. Pat swiftly pulled broadside to him, hooked his hands under the old man's armpits, and heaved him up, balancing his shoulders on the gunwale for purchase, pivoting the trunk and matchstick legs onto the gunwale, gently lowering him limp onto the floorboards. Assured that the old man was breathing and not bleeding, Pat lightly ran his hands over the body. He felt no bones protruding. Then he looked again at the general site of the disaster for signs of the others. He rowed around and around the area, circling in ever larger circles. At last, as a wave rose, he saw something red. He came upon another body, his friend Paddy. The water all about was stained incarnadine. Leaning over to grasp Paddy's arms, Pat discovered Paddy, his pal, had no head. He left him there. A line he'd heard in Mass rumbled through his swirling mind: "Let the dead bury the dead." Mr. Cadogan groaned.

Pat rowed slowly amidst the debris, splinters of wood, tangles of nets, a can of oil, all that remained of the *Roving Swan*. When supine Mr. Cadogan groaned yet again, and coughed, and appeared to be shivering, Pat made the decision to return to North Harbour. Wondering if shivering, like swine flu, was contagious, Pat felt his own body starting to shake. He rowed for warmth, he thought, he rowed for safety; he rowed fruitlessly for all the mothers in the sad, sad world. And all he had been able to rescue was an old man who had lived his three score years, his four score years — he corrected himself — and then some.

Later he learned that Paddy's body — but no others — had been recovered, along with the shattered nets, among which were found bits of flesh and, here and there, like stray sprat, fingers. Some of the pebble-stone ballast carried by the *Roving Swan* was discovered by school children playing on the nearby island shore.

Paddy was buried in St. Ciaran's cemetery beside North Harbour, but because his body had already been driven past the cemetery by boat, he could not — in accordance with island tradition — receive a memorial service in the church proper. Instead, the service took place in the family's kitchen, followed by a burial service at graveside. His father and his brothers had dug the grave the evening before, twice encountering and collecting the musty crowded bones of other occupants and placing their remains in separate burlap sacks. As Paddy's ceremony neared its conclusion, father and brother discreetly loosened the screws on the lid, lowered the coffin by two ropes, and began filling in the grave. They tidily tucked the two burlap sacks on either side of the new wooden coffin, reburied the old bones as they buried the new flesh.

The modest graveyard was filled to overflow with mourners. So too the encircling paths. Some six hundred people, most of them weeping, stood about, heads down. The majority of the adults, once the fresh earth had been smoothed into a neat mound, walked over to where the bereft families stood together, often simply touching their arms by way of condolence, or patting their shoulders.

Old Mr. Cadogan — with the help of Dr. John Shipsey, and the good doctor's nursing sister — recovered, and, in the few years left him, he would occasionally, over a pint of stout or on Sunday evenings a glass of brandy, tell the story of flying through the air one hundred feet up, and then, like a gannet, of diving far beneath the sea; but unlike a gannet, he'd add, he thought he'd never reach the surface again, so deep did he go "in its innards".

And Pat? When he returned to his parents' farm after the disaster, he saw that Deirdre had farrowed without help. Twelve nimble piglets swarmed over their mother or suckled hungrily at her teats. She lay there passive, stretched out at her long ease as if nothing had happened, nothing at all.

Chapter Seven
The Baltimore Lifeboat

All the time
As we went sailing evenly across
The deep, still, seeable-down-into water,
It was as if I looked from another boat
Sailing through air, far up, and could see
How riskily we fared into the morning,
And loved in vain our bare, bowed, numbered heads.

Seamus Heaney, "Seeing Things"

September 1985. Between 1:30 and 1:50 a.m. came call to Baltimore: ship struck Mizen. Lifeboat needed. Foggy, light southeasterly, no visibility. Ship foundered rock north side lighthouse. Dark. Cliffs. Lighthouse keeper can shout down to people; faintly hear them; can't see or reach them from above. Cold.

Requisite crew assembled, off steamed *Charles Henry*, 9 knots per hour, 18 miles destination. Steamed past invisible Cape. Once at Mizen, saw nothing. Fired flares illuminated area. Spotted one rubber dinghy and life raft. Dinghy, one person aboard, rowed to lifeboat. Four in life raft. Christy Collins, coxswain, recognised John Stafford, saluted him, exchanged recognitions. Shortly all five aboard *Charles Henry*. Wet and chilly. Dinghy and life raft brought aboard. Yachtspeople in blankets journeyed back to Baltimore. Other than Stafford, crew didn't know who aboard. Mizen lighthouse keeper called again, requested name of yacht on rocks. Given info. Ten minutes later Mizen called again, requested spelling of yacht. Information exchanged. Disbelief. Now informed, crew member Liam Cotter wished Charlie Haughey belated happy sixtieth birthday. All safely arrived Baltimore 5:30 a.m. Heavy fog. Local accommodations ready. Mission accomplished.

Two years later Kieran Cotter, one of the lifeboat's crew that night, recognised by one of those rescued. "Ah, hello Kieran! You were on your way from a wedding and I from an encounter with the Mizen last time we met."

In late November 1986, while responding to the sinking *Kowloon Bridge*, the same *Charles Henry* came off very heavy sea, sustained structural damage to hull. Successfully repaired, but routine survey in 1987 discovered rot in bilge. Lifeboat immediately condemned, replaced by ex-Ballycotton lifeboat *Ethel Mary*. An interim measure, she had been a stand-by. Need immediately recognised for new lifeboat. Took $10^{1}/_{2}$ to 11 months to construct *Hilda Jarrett*, lifeboat presently in use.

She could have rescued Charlie Haughey and friends in half the time. A 47-footer, member of the Tyne Class, she has 2 Detroit diesel engines, 425 horsepower each; travels 18 knots per hour, consumes 42 gallons of fuel per hour, constructed of steel, radius of c. 100 miles. Cost in excess of £600,000. Built on Isle of Wight in 1987, commissioned early 1988, she arrived Baltimore mid-February 1988. Crew members visited headquarters in Poole, Dorset, for training week prior to her sailing for Baltimore.

The *Hilda Jarrett* reaches Cape's North Harbour in 20 minutes, the Fastnet in 30. When asked if there was any weather in which she couldn't function, Kieran replied firmly, modestly, "I don't think so."

Since 1919, when Baltimore received its first RNLI lifeboat, 187 people have been rescued — as of April 1993. Mandatory practice manoeuvers are held at least once every two weeks, unless rescue missions intervene. They count as manoeuvers.

With a pool of twenty-three to twenty-five stalwarts in Baltimore to call upon, the volunteers have sometimes launched the lifeboat within 4 minutes of the time their beepers go off. Eight minutes is the

Baltimore Lifeboat in North Harbour.

Lifeboat Day 1993: (Left to right) Margaret Cadogan, Sean Cadogan, Charlie Haughey (former taoiseach), Joe Walsh (Minister for Agriculture) and Paddy Burke.

average time it takes them to come from whatever they're doing and assemble aboard. The coxswain and mechanic are involved in every operation, and the first 4-6 others who arrive constitute the rest of the crew for a given mission. All volunteers have proven sea experience. Presently, one woman belongs to the pool.

On Lifeboat Day 1993, I watched the *Hilda Jarrett* bring Charlie Haughey in to Cape to give celebrity status to the day. With thanks to money raised on lifeboat days, the *Hilda Jarrett* will shortly be receiving a DECCA Navigation System, known as GPS, or Global Positioning System, which operates by coordinates provided by on-line satellite.

While Charlie Haughey's rescue proves one of the most dramatic, Kieran particularly remembers a rescue in 1992, one he believes sticks in the minds of the crew as well. The call came in Sunday morning, around 6:00. Valentia Radio ringing. Picked up SOS. Proceed toward the Stags. Life raft seen in water. Distress signal originally received by fishing boat.

Individual beepers gave the alarm. Lifeboat launched down slipway. Powered off. Shortly crew discovered life raft — empty. Then spotted one person on rocks. Just one. They knew *Ontranto* had had two aboard. One survivor. They could see the tips of mast and wheelhouse sticking up from where she had sunk.

What memorable relief to discover second fisherman lying down, sheltered by a plastic fishbox.

Such are the memories dreams aren't made of.

On Lifeboat Days, and at intervals throughout each year, I've watched the *Hilda Jarrett* purr out of North Harbour. No sooner does she reach the outside mouth of the harbour, than she takes off, a cascading mountain of white wake obscuring the boat herself until she settles down. With a smooth deep-throated rumble, she knifes across Roaringwater Bay. No wonder residents of Cape, visitors, fishermen, sailors all sleep easier knowing she's always ready to be of assistance in an emergency. She's Cape's lifeline, ship of last resort.

Chapter Eight
Fishing by the Fastnet

The wind that round the Fastnet sweeps blows in all its fury and in all its gentleness along the entire coast from Cork to the Mizen Head, and makes itself known in no uncertain terms to every yachtsman, every fisherman, every mariner who sails these seas, and there are few among them who have not the healthiest respect for it ... The gods that rule the seas are no playthings for us mortals.

John M. Feehan's *The Wind that round the Fastnet sweeps*

The 34 foot MFV *Katsha* rendezvoused with us at The Bull's Nose, Cape Clear Island, 11:00 a.m., and off we motored, Fastnet bound. On board were two Englishmen, an Irishman, a Canadian, a Swiss, an American. Normally, our skipper said, between 10% and 20% of the deep-sea angling crowd are women, but not today: We were all men, boys at heart.

The late June sea resembled more a dreamy mill pond than a lake. Not a puff of air, not a noticeable swell. Manx shearwaters, flying in tight formation, zoomed past so closely above the still water that we couldn't see their underwing lightness alternating with their black tops; the occasional storm petrel darted toward us, veered off, friendly curiosity satisfied; kittiwakes, herring gulls, and black-backs accompanied us, knowing our sort and waiting for the freebies. Gannets flew high overhead in their relentless east-to-west journey. We spotted seal, dolphin, porpoise.

Four miles west of Cape's Bill, *Pointanardatruha*, the southernmost piece of Irish *soil*, and five hundred yards northeast of the solid *rock* of Fastnet, we cut throttle and drifted, six sets of feathers expectantly thrown overboard. To the west lay the Mizen, with Brow Head precisely etched against it. In the extreme clarity of atmosphere the houses of Crookhaven and Schull shimmered. Hungry Hill and the mountains of West Cork seemed sleepy in the dazzling light. Behind us, like a turtle, rose the rugged carapace of Cape. But, our feathers jigging, we had little time to fall into trance.

Within seconds the first fish flopped about on deck; the first lines became inextricably tangled. The skipper coolly moved from fisherman to fisherman, explaining how to work reels, unhooking fish, replacing lost weights, sharing technique and lore. In what seemed minutes we had filled over a standard box with coalfish and pollack, some with estimated weights of five to six pounds. In came a five-pound cod, a dainty, slippery ling, a wrasse with air bladder blown. But no mackerel.

We had hoped for mackerel, for then we'd have one of the best baits for other fare, conger, blue shark, porbeagle, those formidable denizens of the deep. Finally one of us pulled in a lone mackerel, as small as a sand eel. Cheers went up. "Where there's one mackerel, there's more!" an aficionado cheered. But the mackerel proved downright uncooperative. That tiny fellow was a maverick, not the vanguard of a shoal, an iconoclast rather than a following sheep.

We stopped drifting and, using the electronic gear, located a welcoming deep hole in which to bottom fish. We dropped anchor, made certain it caught. Then we sliced up the coal fish, baited single sizable hooks with bloody flanks. And waited for the monsters to take the bait and run. How ready we were to strike.

The chaotic whirling excitement of catching bait was replaced by the quiet pleasure of being at sea, waiting. While feeling the line rocket to the bottom under the governorship of our controlling thumbs, we'd observe the ever-changing Fastnet. What was life like there one hundred and fifty years ago, in its youth? In the days before generators, what was it like to be stationed there for three months at a stretch? The intriguing sprawling base structure spurred romantic dreams. On one side, from a variety of locations, stone stairs ran up into the bowels of rock and tower. I imagined a vertical labyrinth. Fifty-foot breakers thundered against the citadel.

Occasionally the dreamy spell was broken by someone pulling in a dogfish, or a lesser dog. The much maligned rock salmon became the butt of jokes. Not even a spur hound wagged his tail before gracing our table. Occasionally someone felt dead weight, perhaps a conger refusing to budge far from his lair, and succeeded in lifting something ten or twenty feet off the bottom, but then the line would go discouragingly slack. One mildly dead weight was brought up beside the boat, but before we could gaff it, the father of all crabs wised up and drifted nonchalantly back to his underworld kingdom.

The skipper served tea, the guests shared biscuits, the gulls feasted on tired bait and the guts of fish worth cleaning. We weighed anchor and returned to drifting and feathering. Jack Sprat! We struck a hungry shoal of our old friends, Mr & Mrs Pollack and their extended family. Six fishermen lifted full lines over the gunwales simultaneously. No wonder fish can multiply, someone quipped. The fish we didn't need would become bait in Baltimore lobster pots.

As the poet Blake recognized, "Not enough or too much!" We felt sport slip into slaughter. We had become jaded.

Then one of the Englishmen, a connoisseur, a man who has had his fish photographed by angling magazines and has set British records, shifted to a single lure, a piece of black plastic three-quarters of an inch wide and six inches long. When we saw the size of the Grampa Pollack he landed, we changed from feathers to fake eels, anything that vaguely resembled his. *We* were the sheep, not the mackerel!

And then it was time to motor back. We thought it was, well, maybe as late as three; but five o'clock, five thirty, never. How strange that all our watches had speeded up together. As if on cue, our arms, too, suddenly told us it was time to knock off. Funny how that little sinker, brought up time after time, and two or three fish weighing a pound each (if you must know), brought up time after time, tire one out.

While the macho in me said he couldn't wait to be dropped off on Cape and retire to a pint at Paddy's, the truth in me said rather peremptorily that I was to bed early, no ifs ands or buts, no time to tell the story of the one that got away.

And sure enough, soon I was bottom fishing in the land of dreams, a halcyon day for my lure.

View from Synge Pasture.

PICKING ASPARAGUS TO DOLPHINS

I pick asparagus to dolphins,
let me tell you why:
The smallest pasture of the townland I named Synge,
the old Irish name mute with the Feneens.
One tenth of an acre, it overlooks South Harbour
and due south on out to sea.
Were I ever to build a hunkered-down house,
for us,
I'd place it beside Synge,
picture it perfectly related to the sea.

Any tourist with a camera up our road
stops there — and clicks,
and I click too,
the F-stop in my eye ever ready
for my heart's film.
Were it developed at my death
you'd find a leitmotif of harbour view,
and you.

I pick asparagus to dolphins,
let me tell you why:
Seven trenches dug, I parked the tractor beside
Synge's wall
and forked over fork on fork of humus-black
rotted goat manure, some two tons' worth.
Packing the clingy, worm-rich dung,
pulling in the earth,
mounding it,
spread-eagling the asparagus crowns out
over each of the forty-nine mounds,
covering the stringy roots,

I was half-way through before I took a break.
There, where the inner harbour widens suddenly between
Black Rock Point and Spanish Smugglers Cave,
I zoomed in on a herd of dolphins
frolicking back and forth that quarter mile.
After half an hour, I capped my lens, went back to work
every few minutes looking up, focusing,
and they were there,
rhythmically surfacing, arcing, diving
down, ten fifteen dolphins filling me with peace.
This year that asparagus will be mature.
I pick asparagus to dolphins
and to you.

Chapter Nine
Farming

[Cape Clear] contains about fourteen hundred acres of land, some of which is very elevated, and the far greater part extremely rough, shallow, and infertile, wholly incapable of producing trees, and furnished by nature with a poor covering of heath and creeping furze. The comforts even of fuel, so generally found in rude and dreary regions, are here wanting, the inhabitants being compelled to resort to the most convenient shores of the neighbouring bay for a supply of that necessary article. Under all these disadvantages it supports a population, computed to amount to at least twelve hundred souls, who are so far from considering themselves in a desolate or unenviable situation, that they fear no punishment so much as an expulsion from their favourite island.
Rev. Horatio Townsend's *General and Statistical Survey of the County of Cork*, 1815.

Farming on Cape differs little from farming elsewhere in Ireland — except for the hardships the sea-girt, exposed location, stony soil, uneven hilly terrain, and tiny fields intensify. Farmers raise cattle rather than cash crops; most land when not outright scrub is pasture; highly fertile areas, with topsoil measured to a depth of fifteen feet, do exist, but as the exception. While the best land can support one head of cattle for every two acres, most farmers allow between three and five acres per head, and some farms, such as mine with sixty-three acres, are unsuitable for more than about one head per eight acres.

Back in the early seventies, when the bottom dropped out of the cattle market, islanders tended to hold their cattle rather than sell. Cape's 1578 acres at that time supported around five hundred head of cattle. And back in the thirties, I have heard, when the English "blockaded" Irish ports through tariff wars, Cape's cattle population may have swollen to some seven hundred head.

Today the number of cattle on the island averages around three hundred. There's one herd of about forty goats, the odd donkey, horse, pony, and goat scattered about, desultory talk of deer farming, and until recently a flock of some seventy sheep. While Cape cannot lay claim to being in the vanguard of modern farming techniques — it

To mart.

has, for example, no computerised milking parlours — it makes do with low horsepower equipment appropriate for its small fields. Farmers vociferously disagree as to whether the Massey Ferguson or the David Brown does the better job. Few fields are tilled for crops other than potatoes, turnip, fodder beet, rape, oats, barley. Almost every family has a kitchen garden. While in the last century every family on Cape had its own pig, today there's not a pig on the place — except for Nell's Mildred.

Some farmers have stopped making hay even if the sun shines and instead cut silage, thus saving themselves tedious weeks of repeatedly tossing the same hay when the weather proves "dodgy" or downright uncooperative. Here and there heavy-duty black plastic sheeting, weighted down with car tires, covers the summer's take, often mixed with molasses. But other farmers, partly because the stonewalled fields rarely exceed three acres and the quantity of hay to cut remains limited, continue the old ways, constructing cocks and finally reeks, ricks, hay stacks. While it's the rare farmer who still wields a scythe, cocks dot fields in middle summer, and then reeks — usually covered with fishnets weighted with stones — come to nestle beside a sheltering shed or barn. But more hay is baled and stored in barns than is piked up to the man arranging the forkfuls and stomping about on top of the growing reek. Cape may not be in the vanguard, but old ways are — sometimes sadly — slowly giving place to new. I know only one farm which still ploughs behind a pony.

The following two accounts, one personal, the other (Chapter 10) fictional but based on personal experience, will provide some dramatised picture of how the island location complicates the life of the independent Cape farmer.

*****

Having heard that the process of going from Cape to The Mart in the mainland towns of Skibbereen or Bandon differs dramatically from a mainland farmer's routine, I rose early one spring morning to witness the proceedings.

On the way to the main pier at North Harbour, where the boat loading takes place, I noticed that neighbours had been before me, for their cattle had left unmistakable traces along the narrow lanes, the various exits from which were blocked with Rube Goldberg creations: empty molasses barrels, miscellaneous timber secured with blue string to concrete pillars, dilapidated galvanised gates I'd never before seen shut, some with signs in Irish and English I deciphered as "Keep closed by order."

Within sight of the pier, but out of shouting range, I came upon a group of cows heading home, and thought that to be of assistance I'd turn them back. They were stubborn, however, and immediately broke through a fence rather than reverse direction. Suddenly they were in an unmown field. I had unwittingly complicated the situation. Finally my wife and I succeeded in driving them out, but again they went homeward instead of seaward. Seeing wild gesticulations from the pier, which I interpreted to mean, "Stop them at all costs!", I breathlessly managed to get in front of them and positioned Nell at the gap into the now trodden field. But they broke by me and trotted off down the road to the distant Glen. There was no way I could get in front of them for a quarter of a mile.

Wet with dew and sweat from scrambling though the high grass, sneakers soggy, camera dangling awkwardly from my neck, I wondered what to do next, when a neighbour came up and explained to me that those cattle had been "sucker bait", meek trained cattle he had placed at the head of his herd as he drove all eight down to the harbour. The "sucker bait" he had then intentionally turned loose, knowing they would mosey home, while the ones he wanted to sell were penned balin' wire style at the end of the pier.

When we arrived at the pier, the group in front of us were vainly trying to herd three heifers toward the mailboat berth: one brown maverick broke away and dashed back, frisky as a gambolling lamb, determined as a mature rambunctious bull. In our feeble way we too tried to block her path, but she swept by us with the disdain of a locomotive, veered off the pier, shot off home. I could have sworn I heard her say, "See you next Wednesday, chump!"

Twenty-two cattle and seven goats, finally, were cordoned off at the end of the pier. Farmers and the ferry's crew, some holding metal gates, constituted the movable pen. A sling was made ready, the boat's hydraulic lift put in motion, and one large beast found herself miraculously flying. Once she had been deposited on deck and secured by halter and rope to one of the ship's bollards, a group of four was herded toward the shipside's open door. Although the tide was in, there was still a decent drop, and the cattle balked. How they balked: all sixteen legs braced.

One typical creature had four men working her over. Someone pulled the halter, someone yanked the tail, someone else was walloping her with the standard piece of plastic hose, and yet another pushed against the rump. Manure and curses were flying about, both thick. Her knees buckled as she went in, but she righted herself quickly. As the men turned for the next, the stubborn critter bolted and sprang out again amongst great shouting and pandemonium. I was assured that, since she'd already been in, the next time would be easy

Driving cattle.

53

as duck soup, and sure enough, a little tap and a yank on the tail did the job lickety-split.

The scene repeated itself the requisite times, but, in this battle at least, mankind had the upper hand. After three quarter's of an hour's sweat and struggle, cattle and goats were aboard, carefully scrunched together, tied, ready for the sea leg of their journey.

Farmers walked down steps to the sea to rinse their hands; a mate efficiently hosed the skid marks and general muck off the pier; groups sat about relaxedly having a smoke and chat; a few in boiler suits stood on the bridge observing their livestock. When the tourists going out began to arrive as nine o'clock approached, they couldn't discern that anything out of the ordinary had taken place that morning until they saw the cattle diffidently huddled in the stern.

I queried a few farmers about the difficulties of "The Mart". While islanders may be at a disadvantage because of the trouble and expense of the sea journey — the herding, loading, off-loading, and loading again in Baltimore, all the extra transportation — they also have an advantage: buyers know that Cape cattle have an earned reputation for being sturdy and healthy. They have to be strong to make it out here; and the island location protects the cattle from diseases, most of which spread more easily from herd to herd on the mainland than on Cape, where the very geography places a health control around the cattle, making monitoring simple.

A quiet day. (Courtesy Mrs. Kieran Cotter).

While a Cape farmer may occasionally have to sell at a price he or she doesn't like rather than go to the trouble of bringing the cattle back in to Cape, the quality of the cattle often sets a premium price.

Even with my Yankee city slicker's insouciance, I've noticed that mainlanders occasionally object to hearing yet another story of island hardships. But having seen how much work is involved in just getting cattle onto the ferry (let alone off three hours after their breakfast), island farmers have my full respect for the extra problems their location entails. A fanciful wag tells me that mainland farmers would appreciate the difficulties were they to imagine having to buy and sell their cattle at West Cork's only remaining mart, The Harbour Mart of Cape Clear Island!

Chapter Ten
Making Hay

Of all implements, the pitchfork was the one
That came near to an imagined perfection:
... He loved its grain of tapering, dark-flecked ash
Grown satiny from its own natural polish ....

Seamus Heaney, "The Pitchfork"

Micheál had worked as a journeyman builder on the continent all his days, in Brussels, in Rotterdam, in den Haag. He had never aspired to being a foreman in the Irish construction company, content instead to follow instructions, content to carefully lay every brick as neatly and exactly as if he had been constructing his own house for all those years, and not high-rise, low rent apartment blocks. Now that he had his little pension, he could live out whatever time he had left him where he had grown up, and where he most wanted to live.

His deceased aunt's cottage suited him fine and in half a year he'd replastered the walls, inside and out, having knocked the old plaster off with a hammer, occasionally assisted by a stone-chisel. He'd replaced the rotten window frames with teak, which he'd first anointed with linseed oil and one-quarter part turpentine before sealing with Cuprinol. He'd lifted the old flags that, back in the late nineteenth century, had one night grown legs and walked away, all over the island, from where they had rung round the British lighthouse. Then he'd dry-coursed the parlour and kitchen, and replaced the flags just as they had been before, although now they didn't bleed when the glass dropped. He'd turned and re-pointed the Welsh roof slates; he'd installed a south-facing Velux window in each of the three rooms upstairs, a guest room, a study, and his bedroom.

Where the ramshackle lean-to shed had been on the west gable, he excavated, then built a one-storey extension for the utility room and bathroom. Not a wire showed, not a pipe. The flue drew better than ever even though the chimney now had a bulky backboiler in the

Hay fields.

fireplace. The path to the house from the road he'd restored to its pristine state: its top layer consisted of the traditional white quartz stones, two to four inches in diameter. Hadn't they always kept the fairies at a respectful distance? The escallonia hedge he'd cut way back, giving the apron of yard a clean, tidy look. At the very last, he'd painted the house with a weather-shield white emulsion.

But as Micheál stood beside his finished cottage, feeling a quiet satisfaction in his handiwork, he began to wonder again what to do with the fifteen-acre farm. Should he bring it back to life and farm it himself, or should he rent it out to his neighbour and spend his time simply puttering? It was good land, some of the best land on Cape, low, sheltered, friable land that could support four cows and still allow him to plant his largest field of three and a half acres to fodder beet, oats, potatoes.

Just then Conchubar, donkey's years back a playmate, a pal at the island's segregated school, drove up on his tractor. "Micheál boy," he called, "How ye keeping?"

"Well," answered Micheál, "well! As fit as a fiddle like and as lazy as a hog."

Micheál walked out to the road, rested his hand on the top of the left back wheel of the David Brown. "What's on your mind, Conchubar?"

"Isn't that it exactly, Micheál, exactly now. We've no time no more for talk, no time a-tall, a-tall. Don't it make the old days grand, the *Meitheals* ...." His sentence faded out.

Micheál nodded, attuned.

"I'm wondering if ye'd be willing to give me a hand with the hay. I'm a bit shorthanded, like, and —"

"Here I am, loitering about, wondering what I'd be doing today, not knowing, see," he motioned vaguely toward his cottage; then he added matter-of-factly, "I'll nip back in the shed for —"

Conchubar recognised the decision made and interrupted, "Has your boiler suit another wearing?"

Micheál looked at him, momentarily lost.

"Better to have nothing loose flappin' in the breeze."

"I'll be with ye in as long as it takes a sheep to climb over a lazy neighbour's ditch."

Micheál knew that Conchubar, whose farm was the size of his own, had been trying to bale for two months. Day after day Conchubar had hand-tossed the mown hay, and, time after time, just before the hay was dry enough to gather into cocks, it had rained hard steady rain. And then, once a dry spell returned, and he'd succeeded in gathering the hay into cocks, it had commenced to rain again, day after day, night after night. Driveways had become mud, cattle crushes knee-deep in muck. Sure the hat of the cock let the water run off, but the cocks had to be turned or the bottoms would rot. So, the cocks made, he had to shake them out with his pike, dry them, remake them. That was the very end of September.

Micheál had been aware of the long process, and had understood why many other island farmers preferred cutting silage and being done once and for all with the blasted hay. But Conchubar was of the old school; he wanted his cattle to have what was natural: "Nothing," he swore, "beats weather-dried hay. I don't want no molasses in my cows' stomachs."

Today was a pet day, a perfect October day for baling what the capricious summer weather had repeatedly forced Conchubar to postpone. A steady dry northeast wind blew, and, as Micheál shook out the cocks in front of the tractor-pulled bailer, he began to feel as though he was participating not in a process but a ritual, a ritual determining whether intensive months of his neighbour's labour were for naught.

Cape sparkled around him. The patchwork fields of the gentle Glen, and of Ballyieragh, alternated the lush greens of after-grass with the sudden russets of autumnal fern. To the north old dimpled Hungry Hill darkened with cloud shadow, and lightened again, and again. To the west the last tip of the Mizen could easily be differentiated from Brow Head. The clear white flash of Fastnet's light seemed to serve no purpose save his trance-like pleasure and their camaraderie. He wielded his pike so as to distribute the light fluffy layers of the cocks into long rows for Conchubar's ancient but trusty New Holland baler to gobble up, pommel into bales, tie with yellow twine, dump randomly back onto the field.

Time didn't matter ... for hours, not until he was on the last row of the first field. Suddenly the tractor began to gain on him, the baler eating and disgorging hay faster than he, its waiter, could serve that omnivorous appetite. Whether he succeeded in speeding up, or whether the power takeoff connection slipped more often than usual, or the spoked pick-up drum jammed against the earth more than had been its wont, he didn't know, but they finished the field in unison, Micheál breathless, and set off for Conchubar's Mary's tea and egg salad spread on fresh buttered scones.

On their return, they attacked the last field, half of it sheaves of oats neatly tied and leaning against each other in stooks, half of it oats mown and lying flat, ready for the raking baler. They had to work up hill to bale the flat oats. The baler jammed frequently, especially on slow turns and uneven patches. Walking beside it, Michéal watched his P's & Q's. Whenever the "finger-pick-up" drum teeth jammed, he

Plough horse: Jimmy by Loch Errul.

heaved up the protective guard bar in front of the drum to release the locked prongs. Not anxious to have the baler test its teeth on his leg, he used his pike as a cane: when he lifted the cranky bar with his left hand (his left leg a base for purchase), he simultaneously planted the pike beside his right foot, thus giving himself balance. No no, he was in no hurry to slip under the guard and be thoroughly chewed out by the master. Next he activated the height control latch so that the drum would clatter back into place, and off they went. Sometimes. On the bumpy steep terrain at the bottom of the field Micheál hefted the bar every few feet.

Conchubar kept his head sharply craned around, watching, ready to stop, back up, start again, stop on a dime. Micheál was glad their positions weren't reversed. Conchubar had to be coordinated and responsible for someone else. All Micheál had to do was follow the rhythm dictated by the baler and keep blinking his eyes to free them of swirling chaff.

The first few bales that landed in the oat field were incongruously of hay, left over in the innards of the baler from the previous field. Then out came a bale half hay, half oats, the hay dark almost grayish tan in colour, the oats golden yellow. They joked about this odd half-and-half bale being a collector's item. Later Micheál noticed that three bales were half-and-half, but failed to find an explanation, unless, he jokingly thought, the baler had independent intestines.

The following day dawned with more of the same dry weather and northeast wind. Micheál, knowing just how heavy light bales could become, set out with Conchubar to stow the bales in two barns. By the time the last bale had been hefted onto the trailer, hefted off at the barn door, hugged, and tidily stacked under cover, Micheál drooped, his arms dangling like long limp ropes. The beauty of the day had disappeared. All he could see were his feet, and they were blurred. He sneezed massively, five, six stentorian monsters in a row.

On the roundabout way home that evening, Micheál and Conchubar stopped for a pint at Paddy's. In no time Micheál's vision cleared, his spirits were restored, his appetite whet for supper, and, somehow, they didn't know how, business is best done when no one tries to do business – it was settled. They'd try working together another half-dozen, dozen times and, if all continued to go as smoothly as this time, why, old school chums, they'd, yes yes yes, work their farms together.

Oat cocks above South Harbour.

COW

On the lane to the island post office what
slows me down and finally stops me on the verge
but a single cow ambling along
with her head stuck through a gate.

The gate spreads the width of the lane
and cow keeps sauntering along lackadaisical.

By the time I've undone my knapsack
watched two spilled white letters flutter
out the passenger door into pancake flop
retrieved and wiped them on my jeans
and only then mounted my awkward zoom
why she's disappeared around a bend
and by the time I've reached the bend
coming at me is a herd of twenty cattle
escaped from a stick-wielding disgruntled ambling sentry
once stationed by the post office drive.

Now I understand: they've been forced out
of their usual haunts and channeled toward the cattle crush
because today's the Tuesday
the mainland vet checks for tuberculosis.

In the ditch beside the road around the bend
lies the rusty gate, and now, returning *en masse*,
my whichever cow must mosey incognito past.

I've lost my shot of shots
but cannot doubt on days like this
an islandwide sense of incongruity
I cannot for the life of me dismiss:
I wonder if I don't wear a rusty gate around my neck
for the delight of some other kind of gawking creature.

Chapter Eleven
Christmas on Cape

The peculiar violence of the gales, by which this island is assailed, may be conceived from the following circumstance. All the signal towers on the coast are necessarily placed upon very exposed situations, and of course built in the strongest manner. That of Cape was so rocked and shook by a tempest, a little after its erection, that the lieutenant of the tower, familiarised as he was, by his profession, to the raging of the storm, was so alarmed as to entertain serious thoughts of abandoning his post.

Rev. Horatio Townsend's *General and Statistical Survey of the County of Cork,* 1815.

keptical friends from around the world, and particularly friends from the mainland of Ireland, regularly comment: "That's fine and dandy that you live on Cape during the summer, but how can you manage the winter, the gale season? You won't be able even to think what with the howling of the wind. And you won't want to dare the outdoors, what with the lashing and hammering of the rain. No thank you!"

Having spent twenty-five Christmases in Switzerland, and the twenty-eight before those in the States, I can sympathise with their imagining that our first Christmas on Cape would be our last in Ireland. While we wouldn't want to eat wind as a steady diet, nor shave with salty scud every day, nor try to sleep with hail and sleet and howling gales hassling the reindeer, we feel a new Christmas tradition has been started, and we intend to burn candles in our Cape windows every Christmas Eve henceforth.

For two and a half weeks seldom did the wind drop below Force 8; seldom did it gust over 60 mph; seldom was Paddy Burke's pub not sociable of an early evening, and when it wasn't it was already closed. Between inky squalls we took daily walks up top but well back from the cliffs, having heard tales, once judged apocryphal but no longer, of how sheep can be picked up and tossed easy over, like eggs in a skillet, by that bleating gust.

On our lighthouse perambulation, the wind was blowing so hard that, with mouths tightly clamped shut, it found odd openings, our nostrils, and blew in fiercely, creating drafts down our throats and activating secretions of phlegm. Never (in thirty years) have I heard

Winter twilight.

Nell hawk, let alone so often, or so well; never have I been blown off course so regularly, sometimes unable to luff for twenty-five stumbling feet through furze and heather.

Waves mountainous rushed by the island, house-high, seemingly day after day. Slates from our cottage roof, joined by those of a few other exposed houses, decided to vacation in the Scillys. Tightly sealed windows became sluices for freely-flowing canals of horizontal rain. Hail stones would suddenly pound down, the roof and walls and windows their nighttime bodhrans. If you were caught out, as we were, all you could do was huddle down, turn your back to the wind and stones, pull the anorak hood over your head, wish you were in Florida, and hope the stones wouldn't grow into golf balls. The sting through a pair of heavy-duty blue jeans I still imagine; luckily the welts subsided as fast as the stones melted.

Thunder we heard almost every day; lightning we sometimes saw; black gusty squalls rose ominously in the west forcing us to cover and cower behind the closest ditch and hope the lightning would hit elsewhere, and I, no Ben Franklin, delight in adding, it did. But the gulls and choughs and oystercatchers (twenty-two we spotted in one sheltered pasture) and curlews and shags didn't care a hoot. Nor did we, really. The weather's the weather; you go with it. And without weather, well, we, Northeastern taciturns, might lack for a topic beside the fire in Cotter's Bar.

What did we learn? Over Christmas, Cape isn't a place for

Bollard and hawser (Photo by Kate Sawyer).

badminton; one lob and the bird would alight in the next townland, out of bounds according to our house rules. Seriously, utterly, we learned to respect "the draw". We'd often heard reference made to "the draw", over the course of five previous summers on Cape, but we never quite believed in it, having often paddled our canoe around headlands and in and out of caves and, in sometimes frightened innocence, a few hundred yards south of South Harbour, out into the sea. We never met "the draw", although occasionally we watched a tidal current running into the wind and creating a stretch of loud choppy water about three hundred yards wide and miles long. But no draw.

Still, we listened to the stories and gradually came to sense some mythical beast. Well, it's "hour come round at last" in December, and it was no slouch. We saw the boiling draw rush in and out of North Harbour; we heard it roar; we watched the *Naomh Ciaran* battle it regularly over a two week period, during which the boat could make brave but sporadic, darting runs out and in.

The hardest and most dangerous part for the boat was, to our amazement, not out in the giant seas, but in the harbour itself — because of the draw. The white water created by the draw was like a raging river, but a river that could run both directions at once (cross currents), out toward the sea at the middle of the pier, in toward the land from the end of the pier, sideways swirling further out in North

Harbour. I'd always thought a draw was the same as an undertow, but the only thing "under" about this draw was its underhandedness.

The draw required that the mail boat be brought in and out with hawsers, attached to the pier as a safety precaution. Woe betide the man (called specially to greet the boat) thrown the first rope if he missed it, for the draw could suddenly hurl the boat, and in a maelstrom dash it down against deep harbour rocks that, in normal rough weather, are innocuous. Indeed, the draw taught me to appreciate why some islanders believe that a deepened "all weather" harbour (rather than a "fair weather" tidal harbour) is needed before Cape can become fully viable, year round; imagine having your "main road" unusable for weeks, even months, every year!

Inside, in private, we read the books we'd been meaning to read since spring, with Walter Macken's *The Bogman*, Tim Robinson's *Stones of Aran*, and Seamus Heaney's *Seeing Things* taking family honours. Beside the coal fire we raised a wild branch of tree lupine that had grown too large for our miniature herb garden, trimmed it with a few red candles and ornaments we had brought with us.

When the kitchen flags began to bleed, we put our feet up, pulled the chairs closer to the fire, and heard stories from neighbors about, of course, the weather, and the banshees of Christmases past, and the lobster bigger round than a large loaf of brown bread and able to leap up out of a bucket of water if you made the mistake of passing your hand over it in the dark.

If Cape doesn't suddenly submerge, we're there for all our future Christmases. We've fettered sea anchors to our legs. There's no place we'd rather be, no better time, no better community time, to be there.

Grace the Night

Soon after supper I stepped outside perhaps
to check the direction of the rising wind, and sniff
the sea, perhaps just to step outside.

I sensed something not amiss but odd,
something out-of-place, so scanned the slates,
checked the chimney, did a double-take
at the gleaming pebble-dash of stars in December's
as yet moonless solstice sky.
And promptly fell to musing: No wonder that

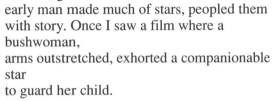

early man made much of stars, peopled them
with story. Once I saw a film where a
bushwoman,
arms outstretched, exhorted a companionable
star
to guard her child.

In the midst of such reverie,
my heart opened to a wild random angel
wanting in: I saw a millisecond thread of
light
from east to west: Palpable, whizzing, white.
It flared over the eastern gable and flashed
out
some thirty degrees above Ballyieragh
and the western sea.

A shooting star flared
in the east, and while it may have disappeared
quicker than I could catch my breath or balance,
it had made its mark across the firmament,
across my inner sky,
and I sorely wished
I had had a grandchild by the hand,
that together we could have shared star, seen
her grace the night. Then it was I felt
an acknowledging little squeeze, and stepped
inside.

Chapter Twelve
A Summer's Day

Here [on Cape] we were on a dream island ...
         John M. Feehan's *The Wind that round the Fastnet sweeps*

*Although Cape can be at its most characteristic with the elements in
turmoil, when a Force 10 hammers the cliffs and cottages, when a
draw prevents the mailboat from daring the harbour, a sunny windless
day in high summer suits tourists and islanders to a T. The following
account may give an idea of such an idyll.* CK

Awizened islander, his black beret perched debonairly on his
pate, his baggy black wool pants secured with twine, saw me
looking wistfully out to sea. He teased me with some Irish
words he knew I didn't understand, and, quietly in English, added,
"Can you smell them?"

I waited, lost. Luckily for me, he continued this enigmatic
conversation. "Sometimes you can tell they're here by the calm
streaks in the water from their oil. But ye look as though ye've a good
nose. Some of the old men, the old men with grey beards who knew
everything about the ocean, they could be smelling them from
anywhere, even the middle of the island."

I remained lost and had to ask for clarification. "Ah," he
exclaimed, "I thought ye were a fisherman: I mean the mackerel."

The mackerel. Yes, I had been thinking of going fishing that day; I
was wondering if mackerel were about; I wished I knew the signs; and
this man, whom I'd never seen before, could read me the way he
could read the sea.

The first mackerel I ever saw I couldn't identify as mackerel. I
grew up in the Finger Lakes of upstate New York, and knew the ways
of small-mouthed bass, pickerel, perch, rock bass, rainbow trout,
sisco. One day, still limited by my freshwater naiveté, but by then a
teacher living in landlocked Switzerland, I came across a picture of a
young man with a string of fish hanging from each hand. What artistry
composed the graceful green-gold skeins of fish, the squid-shaped
barrettes in the young man's hair, I wondered.

The picture of the ancient god Kouros, I later discovered, was painted on a Cretan amphora roughly three thousand two hundred years ago.

Now, having had confirmed that mackerel "were in", and romantically intent on catching my own string of fish, I noticed that the islander beside me had lit his pipe, content without further words, smoke billowing aromatically around him. I thanked him for sharing his olfactory wisdom, and shortly set off with rod and dangling lure across heather-covered headland and down through carpets of kidney vetch and clumps of campion to the Bullig, a jagged point at the southeast side of the mouth of South Harbour. The foot of the fjord-like harbour, where I'd listened to the local fisherman, was now almost a mile to the north. Sandy-bottomed, a picturesque anchorage for visiting yachts except, island fishermen emphasize, in a southerly, the harbour began to cast its spell on me.

With famous Fastnet's lighthouse visible four miles to the west and flashing its warning white light, I cast into the hypnotic sea. An hour or two later I suddenly felt a lovely tug, and reeled in my fish. I didn't know what it was. Then I remembered that picture from thousands of years back. Here was the selfsame fish. I cast again, and again, and again, and each time, to my astonishment, I pulled in long thin magically green fighting slivers of fish.

North Harbour in summer.

Since that introduction to mackerel, many's the time I've feathered for them from my two-person canoe, a plastic bucket clamped between my knees. Straight into the bucket I lower the handline's closely grouped six feathers, what as a boy I would have called wet flies, so that they don't abruptly lodge in fingers or the freed flopping mackerel become immediately familiar with the contents of my pockets.

One hot calm summer's day, gentle Father Kelly saw me return, my bucket full. As always, we had a chat full of friendly banter. I asked if he'd like a few mackerel, and in his gravelly voice he replied affirmatively, but asked if I'd slip them through the open window in his kitchen, since he was on his way to lunch with the Irish college students in the Tír na nÓg hostel.

I walked off the wharf to his house and reached through the window to place a share of the catch on his counter. I gave the fish a good shove to make certain they'd be safe, and they shot along the counter past a loaf of brown soda bread, ricocheted off the kettle, and came to rest smack in the middle of the kitchen floor.

On Cape most doors are left "on the latch", and if someone knocks, you simply holler "Come on in!" rather than "Who's there?" But since Father Kelly's door happened to be locked, there the fish patiently waited until his return. That was food for a laugh another day: What with all the miracles that have occurred in a country historically peopled with saints, we shared mock relief that a multiplication of loaves and fishes hadn't occurred in his kitchen that warm day.

South Harbour in fall.

Another summer's day, while out in a dinghy in South Harbour with a Swiss visitor, I saw mackerel shooting out of the water nearby, and then I saw why. A seven-foot blue shark was resolutely slicing back and forth through a shoal, scattering fish every which way. We shipped our oars, frightened of the rather frisky blue torpedo slashing by, gorging on twenty mackerel at a snap, and came to respect and admire the efficiency of a shark at high tea.

My fondest memories of mackerel are from the last two summers. Sitting in our garden, about three hundred yards up from South Harbour, on some of those windless scorchers, my wife and I watch hundreds of feet of surface water suddenly sparkle, turn turquoise as though hit by a gust from above. Swaths of water explode. Time after time we hear thousands of mackerel leaving and striking the water as they initiate yet another sudden change of direction. Each schooling sounds like ten thousand pebbles sown by some invisible giant hand. At last the proverbial penny drops and we understand the term "mackerel boil".

Miracle enough for us is relaxing outside the cottage in high summer. Below us in South Harbour gulls flock in to spear sprat, international yachtspeople anchor, wondering at the hullabaloo, islanders watch from the seawall, mackerel school. My wife and I wait for evening. My friend with the black beret shares a recipe: mackerel, marinated in vinegar to cut the oil, grilled over the open coal fire.

Chapter Thirteen
Birds

In all Ireland, there's no better place for birds.
David Bird, Ex-warden, Bird Observatory

Imagine Romeo at the break of day exclaiming on the song of 3500 larks. Had he been on Cape Clear instead of in Verona, and on October 22, 1990, instead of Michaelmas, 1303, he'd have had his loving ears full.

3500 skylarks sighted on one day; approximately 280 different species of birds recorded on Cape over the last thirty years. To determine why this island is such an ornithological Mecca, I met with Dave Bird, until recently warden of the island's famed observatory, and received bountiful help. First he regaled me with stories of his sea sightings: Sixty leathery turtles in 1989-90, six killer whales in the last two years, two fin whales last year, two sei whales in 1990, and some bottlenose. Once Dave set up his tripod, focused his glass to count the hourly migration of thousands of shearwaters, and saw a whale shoot straight out of the water, all the way up and out. As I listened to his account, the American Ishmael in me wanted to cry out, "There go flukes."

Dave believes, "In all of Ireland, there's no place better for birds." Worried that this statement might border on hyperbole, I later queried Dave's successor, Richard Humpidge, and he replied,

"Cape's the best place in Ireland for birds. Absolutely."

As I kept pressing Dave with questions about why Cape offers such a vantage point, he enthusiastically loaned me a book by Clive Hutchinson of Cork called *Birds in Ireland*. Within this handsome tome I learned that there are significant feeding areas near Cape and Fastnet where cool and warm waters mix, where "cool upwelling water brings nutrients to the surface. These support plankton growth,

Heron in North Harbour.

which provides food for fish and squid populations, which themselves support assemblies of seabirds ...."

Cape, close to the continental shelf, provides the first landfall for wanderers from my home continent. For habitat it offers a freshwater lake, two major bogs (a third was drained recently), protected harbours, a few dense unkempt gardens, hundreds of acres of undisturbed heather and furze, what's called "the alder wood", more fern bramble and gorse than I'd like to acknowledge, and here and there a clump or plantation of brave young trees. It boasts inaccessible cliffs, derelict buildings, out-of-the-way places ideal for nesting, over-nighting, R&R.

When there's a change in the prevailing westerlies, especially when the wind veers to the southeast, then come the continental (sometimes Asian) migrants; the bird watchers rise early in the morning, return at nightfall exhausted and excited, methodically log their sightings, then compare discoveries over a nightjar in Cotter's or the Club. Occasionally a phone call is made to London or Dublin: We've spotted a Siberian Thrush; or a Black-browed Albatross; or a Yellow-bellied Sapsucker; or the Pallas's Grasshopper Warbler; or, in 1993, the first Sardinian Warbler. Within half a day to a day, the island population of another "rara avis" has increased, and sometimes even lines of bird watchers can be seen crossing a nearby pasture for a closer glimpse of a winged rarity.

For "craic" an islander noted for his humour, or, perhaps better put, for his practical jokes, caught a blackbird and touched it up, adding some red paint to the crown, some white to the tail feathers, and released this garden variety to the vicissitudes of Cape. Sure enough, within a day the bird was being stalked, a celebrity; sure enough, within a week, after much scratching of heads, the bird was caught and the prank revealed. I wonder if birdbrained calls went out to London that week?

Converted, out canoeing I spot a flock of puffins on the southernmost point. In the foggy dusk I hear the distinctive cries of twenty to thirty curlew in formation passing over the cottage; gardening I begin to notice the rich brown wrens and some chiffchaffs or a dunnock. Checking the wind I spot a kestrel hovering, near the cliffs I watch the acrobatic playfulness of the choughs in their free-fall somersaults and the white-rumped rock dove beating to his cave. Climbing a neighbour's ditch I spy a sizeable flock of oystercatchers spread out over the pasture, walking the Harbour Road hopping pied wagtails precede me. Every house has its own seagull, or two, perched territorially beside the chimney pot.

Devoted international birdwatchers, not only courageous indigenous sea pilots, have helped to put Cape squarely on a special map. Home to a bird observatory since 1959, the island welcomes the ornithologists who flock to this landfall and stalk about its lanes and gardens and cliffs with their paraphernalia at the ready. Although the "twitchers", as they sometimes call themselves, alight throughout the year, the aficionados particularly come when the island is otherwise quiet, free from tourists; most agree that the best month for birdwatching is October, though some prefer April, some any time they can "get down". The ten-bed hostel that's part of the observatory is sometimes booked full for months at a stretch.

Having encountered scores of birdwatchers since my arrival on Cape, and having been in on a few sightings myself, I cannot think of a better sort of visitor than these devotees. In a way analogous to the students here to learn Irish, birders put the island to a perfect and perfectly innocent use. (Most birders know to shut all gates behind them, to replace any stone dislodged from a wall, to beware that bull in with the cows.) They appreciate the ecology as much as the quiet beauty of the island. No wonder many islanders welcome the birdwatchers with the kind of pleasure that the birdwatchers themselves show welcoming the migrants.

Birdwatchers on Cape Clear.

A Listing of Birds

Common year-round birds: blackbird, black guillemot, chough, cormorant, dunnock, fulmar, gannet, greenfinch, herring gull, hooded crow, jackdaw, kestrel, kittiwake, linnet, magpie, mallard, meadow pipit, peregrine, pied wagtail, pheasant, raven, reed bunting, robin, rock dove, rock pipit, shag, skylark, snipe, song thrush, starling, stonechat, wood pigeon, wren.

Migrants frequently seen: Arctic skua, Arctic tern, blackcap, black-headed gull, blue tit, chiffchaff, collard dove, common sandpiper, common scoter, common tern, cuckoo, curlew, dunlin, fieldfare, garden warbler, goldcrest, great skua ("bonxie"), grey heron, grey wagtail, guillemot, house martin, lesser black-backed gull, little shearwater, Manx shearwater, meadow pipit, pied flycatcher, puffin, razorbill, red-throated diver, redwing, reed bunting, ring ouzel, rook, sand martin, sedge warbler, siskin, snipe, spotted flycatcher, storm petrel, swallow, swift, turnstone, turtle dove, wheatear, whimbrel, whitethroat, willow warbler, wood pigeon.

Uncommon migrants: black redstart, black tern, brambling, bullfinch, coal tit, golden oriole, golden plover, goldfinch, grasshopper warbler, great northern diver, great tit, green sandpiper, greenshank, grey phalarope, hen harrier, hoopoe, Icterine warbler, jack snipe, Lapland bunting, lapwing, lesser whitethroat, little grebe, little gull, long-eared owl, Mediterranean shearwater, melodious warbler, merlin, mistle thrush, Pomeraine skua, purple sandpiper, red-backed shrike, redshank, redstart, red-throated diver, reed warbler, ringed plover, sandwich tern, shelduck, short-eared owl, snow bunting, sooty shearwater, sparrowhawk, stock dove, teal, tree pipit, whinchat, widgeon, woodcock, wood warbler, wryneck, yellow-breasted warbler, yellow wagtail, yellowhammer (bred up to 1991).

Birds rarely seen: aquatic warbler, barred warbler, bar-tailed godwit, black-throated diver, blue-headed wagtail, bluethroat, brent goose, corncrake (bred until mid-1970's), Cory's shearwater, crossbill, dotterel, glaucous gull, great shearwater, greenish warbler, greylag goose, grey plover, hawfinch, hobby, Iceland gull, kingfisher, knot, Leach's petrel, lesser grey shrike, little auk, little bunting, long-tailed duck, long-tailed tit, marsh harrier, nightingale, nightjar, Ortolan bunting, quail, red-breasted flycatcher, red-breasted merganser, Richard's pipit, rose-coloured starling, ruff, Sabine's gull, sanderling, scarlet rosefinch, scaup, short-tailed lark, shoveler, spotted crake, spotted redshank, subalpine warbler, tawny pipit, treecreeper, tree sparrow, twite, velvet scoter, white-fronted goose, whooper swan, woodchat shrike, wood sandpiper.

Extremely rare (vagrants): Alpine swift, American golden plover, American redstart, avocet, barn owl, bee-eater, black-and-white warbler, black-browed albatross, black-eared wheatear, blackpoll warbler, Blyth's reed warbler, bobolink, Bonellli's warbler, buff-breasted sandpiper, Cetti's warbler, Dartford warbler, dowitcher (spp.), eagle (spp.), eider, fan-tailed warbler, gadwall, garganey, goosander, great crested grebe, great reed warbler, grey catbird, grey-cheeked thrush, indigo bunting, lesser yellowlegs, little bittern, little crake, little egret, little shearwater, little stint, little swift, little tern, long-tailed tit, Mediterranean gull, Montagu's harrier, mute swan, needle-tailed swift, northern waterthrush, olive-backed pipit, olivaceous warbler, osprey, Pallas's grasshopper warbler, Pallas's warbler, pectoral sandpiper, pochard, purple heron, red-eyed vireo, red-footed falcon, red kite, red-necked phalarope, ring-billed gull, rose-breasted grosbeak, rough-legged buzzard, Rufous bushchat, rustic bunting, Sardinian warbler, Siberian thrush, Swainson's thrush, white-throated sparrow, woodlark, yellow-bellied sapsucker, yellow-billed cuckoo, yellow-breasted bunting, yellow-rumped warbler.

Chapter Fourteen
Black-Browed

The germ for the following story — the quest for the bird, the ritual burial, the penance — is based upon actual events and is published with permission; the rest is embroidery. CK

To celebrate his thirty-second birthday, Declan took two weeks off to visit Cape Clear Island in hopes of sighting a black-browed albatross. Not one to merely spot a new bird, add it to a lengthening list, move on to another rarity, Declan was of the old school. He could have been reared more appropriately in ancient Sparta than in council housing on a hill just north of Cork City.

He'd visited Cape many times before and always stayed at the bird observatory. He appreciated the simple communal meals before a coal fire, the devotion with which daily sightings were entered in the observatory's log punctually each evening at 9:00.

He began his vigil the morning after arriving on the evening mailboat. Half an hour before sunrise to half an hour after sunset he swept the skies, the cliffs, the tops of waves, and the skies again, always the skies. Separated from all but the most intrepid, he positioned himself on a far point, the Blananarragaun. He was well wrapped in oilskins when necessary, his telescope sheathed in waterproof canvas with little slits at both ends, his favoured light field glasses hung about his neck ever at the ready, his camera and its zoom protected in his knapsack.

The climb out to the point required the kind of care he gave to his equipment. Each step from the crest of the heather-covered promontory down to the goat-track to the lower jagged headland required patience and sturdy treads. The sixty-degree slope allowed no mistakes.

The more or less horizontal trail reached after the descent was comparatively straight forward. While it took fifteen minutes to

Through the Bellows to Blananarragaun.

navigate the final hundred and fifty yards, clambering from ledge to ledge, it was not particularly dangerous in fair weather. Declan felt finely alert in this forlorn place, as though increased risk increased his appreciation of being alive. He had a spot where he set up his tripod, mounted his telescope, stowed his camera out of harm's way but within easy reach. He watched from dawn to dusk. Most committed birders would watch for four or five hours. Declan could do eight without flagging, unless the sea was blank.

Straining without a bird in sight tired the most diligent twitchers after fifteen minutes. He was no exception. A blank sea, a sea empty of the rapid dartings of storm petrels; empty of shearwaters nipping over the waves and offering glimpses first of their underwings, then of their overs; empty of the fast-flying fulmars and the streamlined gannets in V-formation; empty of kittiwakes, the delicate black bills of the immature; empty of dolphin and shark; Jesus, Mary, and Joseph, he thought, a sea offering only a blank was as hard to look at as darkness itself.

He could estimate, some days, that Manx shearwaters were passing at the rate of 10,000 an hour. Storm petrels, the darting sea swallows, danced about, dipping out of sight, reappearing, shooting off at wild angles.

Day four brought the wind the bird-watchers love, a southeasterly. Declan made the descent to the point's path, stopped to watch a seal feeding on a rock close to shore. He moved on, climbed with alacrity from ledge to ledge. Two flocks of curlew flew by. In the afternoon he heard the familiar cry of oystercatchers, and a flock of sixteen beat past, their orange beaks opening and closing as their echoing cries reverberated from the cliffs.

The next day, after he had set up his tripod and mounted his scope, he had no sooner focused three miles out than a minke whale bolted out of the blue, shot straight up until even its tail cleared the water. Declan gasped. The thought crossed his mind that he had been unready.

On the sixth day of his vigil, he saw a feeding frenzy. A quarter mile out, tens of thousands of birds swarmed a stretch of sea. Dolphins rose and fell in the midst. Gannets plummeted, a dainty plume of spray flaring above their entrance points. His favourites the great black-backs, tough greedy devils, made quick jabbing movements with their heads. He laughed. He accepted the slaughter. With his glasses he could see silver slivers of mackerel in the turbulent water. After half an hour, he had dined to satiation. He leaned back into the embrace of his niche for a moment, slept.

When he woke, he knew he had had a dream. He was quivering as he tried to find it, focus on it, zoom in. An hour later he still held on to the knowledge that he had had the dream even though it didn't, wouldn't, reappear. While he was searching the skies for the black-browed, he was simultaneously searching for what he suddenly conceived of as his inner skies, wherein the evasive dream.

He saw four grey herons flying due south, straight out to sea, their massive wings, as if in slow motion, calmly beating. One was immature, lacking contrast between its wing and body colours. What intelligence informed this foray, he wondered. Why should wading birds head due south, with nothing between them and the South Pole? Ten miles out, they wheeled in giant circles some mile in circumference, and then split, one going east, two inland, one west toward the Mizen Head. And he had the dream, as clear and clean as a sighted bird.

Before me flies an Egyptian ibis. She has four young, fledglings, pursued by four ravens. Each raven seizes an immature ibis and tries to fly off, but the weight of the birds is significant, keeping the ravens close to earth. The ravens cannot shoot off quickly but still the mother ibis doesn't know how to rescue her children. I go into action, race after the ravens, batting first one to earth, another, rescuing ibis after ibis from savage beaks and talons. The ravens depart, beaten; the mother ibis collects her brood, and as she prepares to depart she looks at me and says, simply, "Wolf."

Declan felt fine, alone, not lonely. He resumed his vigil.

On the eleventh day, the sea flat calm, a touch of mist rising here and there, he watched the occasional fulmar glide by, its stubby neck suggestive of quiet strength. It followed sea patterns he couldn't spot. Toward midday a herd of porpoise came into sight, swam leisurely east to west, the same direction that seabirds and salmon invariably follow past the point. From the west came a two-person kayak. The man and woman didn't see the porpoise until they were in the very middle of them. Declan could hear the porpoise breathe, hear the man and woman exclaim in the midst of the passing herd. He felt he was near the beginning of time.

On the twelfth day he drew a blank. Again and again he focused out to sea, raised his glasses to the skies, but nothing: *Blankety blank blank blank.* By noon his neck was sore, and where the glasses touched against his eye sockets he felt rawness. Most of all he grew exceedingly tired. *What would a wolf do in this situation?* he wondered. He went back to scanning the skies. Fifteen minutes, twenty, twenty-five minutes he viewed the heavens, the sea. But no go, nothing, blank. At sunset he was exhausted. On the climb off the point, he slipped once and banged his knapsack into a rock. Back at the observatory he discovered that he had jammed a set-screw on his zoom.

The next day he slept late. When he went down to breakfast the tardy birders teased him about his sloth. He had a vertebra out of joint in his neck and he couldn't turn his head to the left. But he teased them right back, banter filling the kitchen. *Declan, how many Sardinian warblers did you see yesterday? None, I confess*, he replied gaily, *but I did spot a pair of yellow-bellied sapsuckers.*

Knowing that his vacation was over the next morning, that he had to be on the 9 o'clock *Naomh Ciaran* to the mainland, he accepted an invitation to go to the alder wood. Someone had seen a Marsh Harrier there the day before .

At supper he heard the news. A black-browed albatross had been sighted out on the Blananarragaun. Kieran now had 236 birds on his list and, he hoped, a good photograph to prove it. The bird had flown in from due south and flown off west, toward the Mizen. Declan congratulated Kieran and quietly retired to bed.

Early the next morning he borrowed a farmer's pick and climbed to the top of the Blananarragaun. He walked west to a knoll above a massive outcropping of stone covered by interlacings of Xanthoria and sea ivory. There, well off the rabbit path just below the crest, he dug a hole two feet deep, a foot square. In the hole he carefully placed his log, his telescope, his field binoculars, in their case, all meticulously wrapped with a piece of black plastic, which he had neatly cut from a sheet blanketing a pile of silage. As he replaced the earth, and disguised the fresh peaty soil with a design of stone and a clump of heather, he spoke aloud in a determined yet relaxed voice: *Wait here for seven years, my gentles. I'll be back. Maybe then I'll be ready for the black-browed. Not until then will I resume this passion.*

He paid his bill at the bird observatory, boarded the 9 o'clock boat. Standing in the stern, diesel fumes passing overhead, he seemed to be watching Cape Clear recede in the distance, but he was intent on those inner skies.

He discovered that he could already turn his head twenty degrees further left than the day before.

The razorbills and guillemots, the shags and terns, they floated in the wake unnoticed. Declan's eyes were elsewhere, on a prerequisite vigil.

From somewhere unbidden he heard an emended proverb repeat itself: *Haste and lethargy are the work of the devil.* He knew. He laughed.

THE GREY HERON OUT OF SOMEWHERE WHO HAD SOMEWHERE TO GO

Across South Harbour, in Coosangaloonig, the chase began,
three herring gulls pursuing one grey heron.
What he'd done (if one need do anything), I failed to see.
They took turns in their attacks, slashing singly through evening air.
He didn't swerve but shrug into moments of evasive augmented
rhythm.

Veering east, crossing the harbour below my perch,
he flew low over the priest's house,
past the school, shrugged beside the master's place, where the gulls
gave up.
As if in collusion, a jagged-winged raven picked up the attacks.
Over another hollow of pastures,
heron shifted direction, powered north, up the Keenleen,
allotting crow no recognition.

Heron simply flew on, over crest, out of sight, leaving behind crow,
gulls, me. I quieted, but first became preposterous, egocentric,
wondering if all that was possibly a gift, a performance,
a parable in flight: Didn't Harbour herself say,
"Brother, why bother about tormentors? Beat on home."

Chapter Fifteen
Back-Paddling

*The cliffs on either side of South Harbour are high and rugged and the
continual lashing of wild seas have sculptured out innumerable caves
on either side where an incredible variety of sea birds make their
home.*

John M. Feehan's *The Wind that round the Fastnet sweeps*

First thing most mornings Jimmy surveyed South Harbour from a
lookout point beside the kitchen garden. Routinely he checked
wind direction, cloud, swell, tide, who was out lobstering; had
his cattle broken through a wall and headed for the cliffs; had the goat
chewed through his tether again; were house gulls Herman and
Hermione still loitering around the chimney pots, or had they gone
scavenging? Being a curious old bachelor, he would lift his binoculars
and examine Ballyieragh, Cumer, the Keenleen, the Glen for signs of
neighbourhood activity, anything unusual, anything out of place.

One recent summer Sunday something was different. He could feel
it, hear it, smell it; it was as if a rare visitor had joined in the general
birdsong, but he, old Jimmy, could identify neither bird nor song.

Slowly he became conscious of the shrill human cries from across
the harbour, spotted the milling flight patterns, followed them down to
water. Hundreds of herring gulls filled the outer harbour, dotting the
surface so profusely that at first he had thought their whiteness a thick
foamline and passed on to other sights. Then he spied in their midst
sudden plumes of spray, the reverberations of gannet dives, one after
another, silhouetted against the cliffs of the outer harbour. Shrieking
their "glebe, glebe, glebe", oystercatchers streaked in tight formation
about the harbour, as if not knowing where to land. The low tide
revealed not only dark swaying clumps of kelp but, he knew, a
carpeting of mussels on the large rocks and a sprinkling of periwinkles
amongst the pebbles on the lower tidal reaches of the two strands. The
oystercatchers would soon select from the daily menu.

Now and then, hoping it a good-luck dolphin, he saw a quick fin duck into the brine, but always, twenty or thirty yards off and half a minute later, a shag surfaced. Ah, he said at last to himself, realising how slow the penny had been to drop, the mackerel are in; anybody who wants to feather to fill a few boxes could do so as quick as Jack Robinson today. A couple hours of flying hooks could fill a freezer.

But he wasn't in a fishing mood, and his moored dinghy needed fifteen minutes of bailing, so he went on to a mundane task he'd been putting off for too many months: he spent the day emptying a shed, shuffling its contents, and then refilling it in a logical rather than a random way. Paints rested beside paints, tools by tools, and, well, miscellaneous by miscellaneous.

Early evening he had finished with the shed and rewarded himself by climbing part way down the fern-infested hill, a project for another year, and settling himself under a rocky outcropping, protected from the gusty backing northeast wind. Before him was the inner half of South Harbour where the gulls were now feeding as though there were no gourmet difference in the world between breakfast, lunch, and dinner. Eggs and rashers could happily follow mince pie, and all be boiled in mackerel oil.

A memory came to him unbidden of the first time he had slept in the master bedroom. His mother had been dead for sixteen years, his father three years longer. Finally he had determined that he would move out of his boyhood room, the smallest in the usual arrangement of three upstairs bedrooms, and move into theirs rather than his

South Harbour 90 years ago. (Courtesy of the Lawence Collection).

sister's old room. He had needed a fireplace himself. He had been developing chilblains, and having a fire through the winter nights might do away with the swelling, the itch. His grandmother's recipe of stewed onions in a poultice had helped, but not enough.

After his first night's sleep in the master bedroom, he had felt as though he had at last taken possession of the family homestead. And, as if to confirm that he had done the right thing, he had literally felt, when he stepped outside to survey the world, and his domain, that first morning, an enormous splat on the top of his head, as though someone had broken a breakfast egg on his balding crown. Touching the spot, his hand had come away dripping. Sailing over the escallonia and hebe hedge, a mischievous herring gull had disappeared from sight. Jimmy had laughed. Gullible he was, he had known, but lucky, too. Not a bad sign for the day. He had made the right move.

The memory dissolved, a wave upon the far shore.

On this particular recent Sunday, nestled there beneath the rock on the fern-infested hillside, Jimmy decided it was high time he understood how gulls fished. He'd been a fisherman much of his life, and travelled the watery world, but he'd never looked closely at feeding gulls. He'd simply taken them for granted. He began to study the seafowl closely with his binoculars. A solitary gull flew nearby, just below him; he could hear the wind in its feathers. Jimmy zoomed in on the gull as the gull zoomed in on his meal. The gull alighted and

South Harbour today.

83

they both went to work.

Jimmy knew the gull wasn't strong enough, despite his evil-looking splotchy lower mandible, to spear and swallow a mackerel; he would have to content himself with sprat. But how exactly did a gull fish for them? Here I am, he thought, sixty-six years old, a retired fisherman, and I don't yet know how herring gulls fish; what kind of world is this, Jimmy?

As his eyes grew accustomed to the shimmering light, the surface dazzle of the water drew his attention. Only then did the next penny drop: Those bits of glitter weren't just ripples but fish jumping. Sprat were running inches below the surface, harried by the mackerel below. The sprat, why, they created the diamond dazzle, both with the tiny bits of water they dislodged and by their own colouring. "Jack Sprat," he exclaimed aloud, thinking of an English fisherman friend's favourite exclamation and of the nursery rhyme, Jack Sprat could eat no fat/his wife could eat no lean! Jack Sprat indeed! The expression took on new meaning as his eyes feasted on what was now the cornucopian platter before him. He smiled, chortled: at sixty-six he'd licked a mystery clean!

St. Ciaran's Church.

Elbows on knees, glasses firmly centred on the scene, he intensified the field of focus so as to include only that solitary gull, *Larus argentatus*, the warden of the bird observatory had once taught him, delighted to find an old fisherman with an ornithological curiosity. Jimmy noticed that when the gull swam headfirst the same direction as the tens of thousands of nimble sprat, he didn't have much luck nabbing them with his sudden thrusts; but when he turned around, and swam backwards, with the sprat jumping in the direction he was back-paddling, he had no trouble filling his gullet with each swift dart of his head. As sedate as he could be, a gentleman of the old school, Jimmy thought, the gull went about his evening meal, all around him silver slivers of sprat breaking water.

Jimmy realised that he had reduced his entire world to one concentrated image of a scavenging gull. He felt inebriated.

Chuckling to himself, he said aloud, "Now there's a way to put Guinness and Murphy's out of business." And then he decided that he, too, would have to learn to "back-paddle". Being in the right place at the right time wasn't enough; it was how you did it that finally mattered, and you did it — he held on to the image of the gull — by "back-paddling".

Later in the evening, he walked haltingly down to the pier to bail his dinghy. The sun was setting, the harbour filling with muted orange-red radiance. On the pier were father and son, returned from feathering. Jimmy struggled to squat on his haunches and chat with his neighbours. He watched their young deft fingers gut a hundred pounds of mackerel, heads and innards chucked unceremoniously into the sea to a growing flock of tussling herring gulls joined now and then by the much stronger and more aggressive black-backed.

He saw himself as a young boy. He wondered if he'd ever done anything like this with his father. He couldn't remember. But then, did it matter? What really mattered, he realised, was that a father and son, any father and son, did it together. And if they could do it while back-paddling, well, the world was blessed.

When he arrived back home, winded from the bailing as well as from the hill, on which he'd stopped rather more times than on his last foray, old Jimmy walked first to his lookout point beside the kitchen garden. He checked wind direction, cloud, cattle, goat. He scanned Ballyieragh, Cumer, the Keenleen, the Glen. All was where it should be. His feet didn't itch. Herman and Hermione were perched on either side of the chimney pot as though they had been up to nothing all the live-long routine day. It was time for eggs and rashers, and bed, in which, that night, he back-paddled for his last time.

Chapter Sixteen
A Canoeing Caper

What Irish man, woman, or child has not heard of our renowned
Hibernian Hercules, the great and glorious Fin M'Coul? Not one,
from Cape Clear to the Giant's Causeway, nor from that back again to
Cape Clear.

Joseph Jacob's collection of *Celtic Fairy Tales*

O ne balmy summer's day, the sea so flat as to barely breathe
even in the amplifying gurgling caves of South Harbour, the
weather locally reported ready to stay in this placid torpid
slumber for a month of Sundays, my son Charles and I launched our
two-person canoe — what we would call a kayak in America — to
venture forth to the Bullig, the southeastern headland at the wide
mouth of the outer harbour.

Not without trepidation. Together, in our freshwater polyester
canoe, we'd never before sallied forth into the ocean. Indeed, we'd
rarely canoed together for half a dozen years, since his mid-teens. But
the grottoes and the tunnel under the beautiful Bullig beckoned; an
adventure together, in Ireland, beside our new family home, beckoned.

We gathered the modicum of equipment: the life jackets lent us by
the Youth Hostel, the safety anchor and long rope to stow in the bow
just in case a surprise wind blew up, a compass should a freak fog
come in, a mirror (on the back of the compass) to signal for help,
helmets. The tide was slack, there were no signs of unusual currents,
no draw. We were quite simply bursting with pleasure at being alive,
and we wanted to stay that way.

The day before we'd seen dolphins lazily cartwheel past the Bullig,
which, too, was a welcome sign, for a gentle grizzled island fisherman
had told me (translating from the Irish) to beware the sea when
dolphins leap rambunctiously and fully out of the water. (Beware the
sea when a rainbow-like halo is seen near the sun. Look out for high
wind when you spy mares' tails in the sky.) No astrologers, we were
nonetheless sufficiently reassured that signs were positive: we were in

The populated side of Cape Clear.

the ascendant.

Off we went, Charles' sturdy shoulders in the bow for the work, my steering years in the stern for the play. In less than five minutes we had entered our first cave, long and narrow and dark, with fresh water dripping from the ceiling making reverberating plunks wherever it hit the quietly luminous sea. Proceeding slowly, tentatively, we probed a hundred yards into Stygian gloom.

Phosphorescent sparkles came from below, yet I had fantasies of myriad bats disturbed in their sleep, creating a Hitchcockian scene, the depths of the cave our belfry. Might this echoing dwelling be home to a giant squid? Silly, these thoughts, even childish; they had come unbidden as we relaxed into this new world, and we shared them, enjoying our own idiocies. Sometimes, I think, you have to be a little crazy so that you don't go downright loony.

We peered about, our vision becoming accustomed to the dark, and edged forward. When the cave narrowed to paddle width, we became cautiousness itself. And as the ceiling became overly familiar, we desisted, worried that that freak wave might suddenly manifest itself, and squash us into the jagged roof. We back-watered, turned, our eyes by then sensitive enough to notice the light bouncing off the floor of the cave, making the depths of the water in an odd way more illuminated, more lively, than the air.

Not consciously claustrophobic, we lingered, taking in the soothing rise and fall of the quiet sea, not greater here than outside, but

87

magnified by the severely limited space and the eerie acoustics.

As if having held our breath while within, we erupted out of the mouth of the cave, feeling free and unbridled. Squinting in the brilliant light, we paddled hard, luxuriating in what we had not known was freedom before we experienced the confines of the cave.

We came opposite the arch sloping down to the Bullig. Some call it a bridge, a natural bridge of stone over to the final spit of rock. Others call it the Bellows, the name I prefer because it has a story in it, as I discovered one blustery day earlier in the year. The wind was up, Force 10, and as I struggled carefully down from the crest of the townland of Glen West to just above the Bullig, I became aware of a savagely increased howling. Finally I understood. When the wind was funnelled through the tunnel, its power intensified, all that wind suddenly forced into less space. The principle of the bellows, leaning quietly against my fireplace, dramatised itself in the wild whirling scene before me.

So Charles and I canoed under the bridge, through the Bellows, and on into the cul-de-sac channel of water on the far side. In a heavy sea this short stretch of water swirls about like a seething cauldron; waves rear up and crash over the point itself, mounds of cascading foam rushing forward. Flakes of scud fill the air, like the alpine snow where Charles grew up. But on this day, with the highest wind velocity no more than a zephyr, the windmills at rest, and the Atlantic swell so subtle as to delude me into imagining that I might be paddling about on Owasco Lake, one of the Finger Lakes in upstate New York and my original stomping ground, on this perfect summer's day, the Bullig and the Bellows were as silent as barnacles.

We reached the end of the channel and held the canoe steady, staring down at the slowly swaying strands of kelp. As the sea breathed, we rose and fell, rose and fell, in a hypnotically languid rhythm. At last, rising from this torpor, we back-paddled, scooted through the Bellows, and shot out into the open sea itself, invigorated, playfully paddling full out, a wake streaming behind us. Before we knew it, we had reached the next point east, and the point after that, points I had climbed down, retrieving sheep for a friend, but had never seen from the sea.

Cape looked so different from this fresh vantage. Here was the tiny island I had hiked and hiked, yet I could barely recognise it through this new perspective. From several hundred yards out to sea, the striations of old red sandstone had discernible patterns, motifs; here they flowed horizontally, there they bolted up vertically, there they were at a capricious, jaunty, 45-degree angle, God's crazy pavement. I was reminded of how artists step back from their canvases to take a gander at the effect of their work, work they know intimately but can't judge without distance. Ah, I thought, I'm glad the Creator stepped back while fashioning the cliffs of Cape.

Charles stopped paddling; I stopped, except for a light dip now and again to keep us straight; we felt around us the intimate sea. Almost at the same moment, we commented on how, in this little craft, snuggled right down into the water, we wouldn't like to venture further out, even on this seemingly safest of days. He asked about the risk we were taking, and I responded that in two minutes we could make a landfall there, or there, and ditch the canoe, if need be. From that moment on we kept landfalls in mind, and in sight.

It was then we realized that we were not exploring South Harbour, but embarking upon the circumnavigation of Cape. Uneasy, certainly not intrepid, we agreed that if anything untoward started to develop, we would make for shore. At the first puff of a north wind, for example, we'd dart into the nearest Coos or small inlet. And we could always stop at the East Landing, or at North Harbour, or at one of the small beaches whose names we were learning, and call it a day.

As we drifted in the silence following our discovery of what we were about, we were surrounded by a wheeling screeching flock of seabirds. They circled us again and again, some twenty to thirty gulls, and while at first we felt strangely vulnerable, after a few minutes, not having been bombed by a great black-backed or a skua, we began to enjoy the excitement and marvel at being their cynosure. Maybe they thought we'd be gutting some fish and tossing inner delicacies. When we resumed paddling, they flew off, disillusioned.

From below, the lighthouse looked looming, but at such a distance. No wonder it wasn't used for long: above 400 feet, where the lighthouse stands, there's frequently a layer of fog that doesn't drop much lower.

I noticed a current tugging at us. We were approaching the notorious and sometimes treacherous Gascanane. For several hundred yards we hugged the shore and watched what happened. Clearly we could power our tiny craft along. We skimmed over the slight choppiness created by colliding tide and current and a touch of westerly breeze. No problem with those shoulders in the bow and no combers. We continued.

What a change. Gone were the cliffs, the colonies of nesting seabirds, the feeling of seascape wilderness. Welcome to domesticity. The northeast side of the island, which we'd examined dozens of times when going into Cape, now was experienced in contrast to the southern exposures, savage, steep, without visible human habitation.

Here, in the northeast end, cattle grazed, farmers tossed their hay, occasional cars and tractors putt-putted about their business, houses and sheds dotted the gently sloping landscape.

From the sea, the dramatic juxtaposition of the south- and north-facing sides of the island gave me pause. I was reminded of one of those horrible books I had had to read as a boy, and to which as a man I often subjected my own students, hoping I'd help them discover not tediousness but basic conflict: *Wuthering Heights*. The south side of Cape was, for me, "the heights", a fitting wild home for Heathcliff, in this world or that; all we could see from several hundred yards out were cliffs, caves, the solitary lighthouse and watchtower complex, two adjoining miniature walled patches way below the lighthouse, steep vast stretches of heather, naught else. The north side, "the grange", sloped down as if a peaceful populated valley where people could be seen going about ordinary activities: there's the church, there the museum, over there the pubs, the safe harbour. Both sides essential to wholeness.

As if teaching us, Cape showed us lovely little beaches we had not seen before even though we thought we had walked the entire coastline. We glided past the entrance to North Harbour, past the O'Driscoll Castle, the Castle of Gold, and then, in the barely perceptible seas, we witnessed ahead massive waves breaking, crashing down, on this calmest of days. A seemingly minuscule rock lay a hundred yards off, and was it ever busy, Grand Central Station.

We gave it wide berth, going much further off shore than usual to avoid threatening cross-currents. Later I asked a local mariner for its Irish name, and for the English translation: *Tonelunge*, Ships' Bottom. Apt.

Halfway between Ships' Bottom and the Bill, Cape's most westerly long peninsula, my heart shot into the cave of my mouth: I saw a shark fin slicing through the water straight for us. As I was about to tell Charles to hold, the shark bucked half out of the water and proclaimed himself, thank you, a Risso's dolphin. Relieved, but still worried that he might bump us, we waited, poised for action. But he had learned all he needed to know with that one reconnoitering cartwheel.

Turning south around the Bill, and about to begin the final leg of our course, we had more than an escort. An entire regatta from Schull was tacking back and forth toward the Fastnet. We found the company of the sailboats comforting. We weren't alone at the most out-of-the-way part of our afternoon voyage.

From the Bill to the Blananarragaun, the western point at the wide mouth of South Harbour, we stayed well out. Here the cliffs were high, jagged, and the water below had an unfriendly aspect. Numerous narrow canyons and crevasses cut into the desolate land; a junked car teetered saliently on a cliff edge; the sea churned heavily around rocky outcroppings. Normally intent on enjoying the moment as well as the goal, I suddenly wished myself in South Harbour, safety.

Charles and I didn't speak but sped along below the cliffs, which seemed higher and considerably wider than when examined from the land. I had a feeling of steady bleakness, brutality. We turned north. We shot past our lobster pots. We entered the inner harbour. We were home. Home meant more than it had four hours before.

Ballyieragh Ruins.

Stone

Once in close shooting lobster pots
by Tradooncleara he
spied a seam of stone straight as a plumb
line,
straight as the gables of the houses
that he builds. He told me where so I
drove the tractor down to the strand
& found the rock: orange, red, gray, a hard
true sandstone falling south.
With the five-foot bar
we quarried stone, four tons of
sharp edged warm face
that stays where it's put
on wet dark beds of cement.
We built a house with stone
we had badgered out of stone at the edge
of the sea.
He taught me not walls but foundations.

Chapter Seventeen
St Ciaran

The most interesting circumstance connected with the history of Cape Clear ... is the fact of its having been the birth-place of St. Kieran, who preceded St. Patrick by thirty years.

Daniel Donovan's *Sketches in Carbery*, 1876

To tell Saint Ciaran's story as story, I have spliced together a multitude of accounts of this pre-Patrician saint, drawing upon Father Mulcahy's "Life of St Kiaran", the Scholiast of Aengus, the "Genealogy of Corca Laidhe", Sir Jas. Ware, James B. Burke's "Cape Clear Island", J.P. Conlon's "Cape Clear Island", Donovan, and various hagiographies. I present the alleged, the metaphorical, and the self-imagined embroidery as fact. CK

In June of the Year of Our Lord 351, Princess Liedania confided to her husband, Lughaidh, that she had had a most strange and confounding experience. She had been standing, lost in thought, beside the single round upright stone just west of the white strand called Finntract, not far from their home.

"Early last night," she continued, her voice quiet but firm, "a dazzling night, with stars so bright I could see shadows cast by our house and by the pillar stone, even though there was no moon, I suddenly saw a sight that made me drop to my knees in trepidation. And then the sight entered into me, and I am wondering, dear Lughaidh, what I should do, and what it all betokens?"

"Tell me, Liedania, exactly what befell you, and, if I'm able, I shall advise you. I too, last night, heard a soft whispering song-like music off the sea, and it filled me with wonder and made me think our farm enchanted. Please tell."

"As I watched the stars, one began to move out of the Plough, becoming brighter and brighter, until it approached me like a luminous small swift bird. Before I could do anything, it was suddenly hovering in the air before me, reducing itself in size but intensifying itself in brightness. And then, to my utter astonishment, light shot into my mouth. Before me was nothing, within me everything. I could feel a pleasing warmth spread through me and feel it still. Were it not for the

North Harbour, 1969 (Courtesy Cork Examiner).

lingering warmth, I'd say I had had a dream, but the kind you remember for a lifetime, not just for a morning.

"There's a time to speak, Liedania, and a time to listen. So I often heard as a boy from the grey beards of Kilkenny. Let us take your experience over east to our chief Druid.

With the Magus they climbed Cape's highest hill, and waited there in the evening silence, as he had directed, until the sun had set. The sky to the west filled with gold, as if becoming lighter rather than darker; the bay below, dotted with its hundred islands, flattened during their silence, and now had the appearance of delicate sheet gold, not unlike the lunula worn by the priest. The scene came together. The wise man spoke:

"Thou shalt give birth to a marvellous son and great will be his character and virtues to the end of the world."

On March fifth, 352, Ciaran was born in the same house where his mother had been born before him, and the angels of heaven attended upon the Princess Liedania, and the orders of heaven baptised Ciaran. And it was not long before his parents and neighbours were amazed by the way animals gently nuzzled him, and birds flew about him. One day, in his sixth year, a kestrel hovered overhead, and suddenly fell upon a nearby wren. The kestrel seized the little bird, flew off, made several swoops, and alighted with the wren now crunched in his talons. Ciaran, moved to pity, cried out, "Kestrel, kestrel, return thy right to me." And immediately the kestrel gripped the wren, and flew to Ciaran, laying the bird before him. And Ciaran said, "Arise, and be made whole", and the bird arose, and fluttered its wings, and flew to its nest in the nearby wall.

When Ciaran was almost thirty, he took leave of his parents, and, intent on becoming educated, and having heard some curious rumours of the Christian religion as practiced in Rome, he rowed to the mainland with three fishermen friends, the sea as flat before them as a beaten platter. In 382 he finally reached Rome, where he spent twenty years and was consecrated a bishop by Pope Celestine. On his roundabout way back to Ireland with his companion Declan, he met a man called Patrick, on the Mediterranean island of Lerins, and, while living and studying together in the same settlement, this Patrick told him:

"Go forth before me, and in Christ's name found a monastery at a well called Uaran."

"And where is that well, Patrick?"

"Here," said Patrick to Ciaran, first touching his own chest, "take this bell with you, and carry it over your shoulder, and when you have reached the well, the bell will ring out for all the world to hear."

Ciaran returned to Ireland, bade God-speed to Declan, and preached the Gospel on his home island of Cape Clear, where he celebrated the first Mass in all of Ireland. One day, with a multitude of birds swarming gaily over his head, he inscribed on the old pillar stone two crosses, the first crosses ever carved in all of Ireland. And then, with the help of Ireland's first Christians, he built a chapel beside the white strand close by his family home.

Cape Christianised, Ciaran set out to preach the length and breadth of the district of Corca Laidhe, or what we now call Carbery. Pleased with the progress of the people, he journeyed next, chanting psalms as he went, throughout the midland counties; and when he reached the Slieve Bloom mountains, he felt a powerful affinity for them. Thirsty, he stopped beside a well at Saigher in Ossory, now called Seirkieran, and then the bell, which he had carried mute, rang out for all the world to hear.

At first Ciaran lived by himself, in the company of wild beasts. Fox, wolf, deer and badger subjected themselves to his rule as if they were devoted monks. With the assistance of a wild boar, whose tusks cut down twigs and grass, Ciaran fashioned for himself a rude hut, the walls of wickerwork, the roof of dried grass, in which nested wren, robin and wagtail. A stream flowed beside the hut, running down from the Slieve Bloom mountains. A little distance from the stream, and over the well, grew a whitethorn bush, with elder and hawthorn beside it. One day, remembering his beloved well on Cape Clear, and recalling the pillar stone on which he had inscribed two crosses, he raised a stone next to his new well. When he had it firmly in place, he laid his hands upon it, blessing it, and to this day one may see the impression of his fingers on this stone.

Ciaran desired nothing more than time to pray to God, which he did even as he went about the routine of the day. Yet he found little time to be alone, for disciples soon discovered his place of retreat. In 402 he founded a monastery at Saigir, from which spot he made one of his most famous prophecies:

"To the progeny of Eiderscel [the O'Driscolls], reign and chieftainship over their race forever and ever."

Not many years after the founding of the see, Ciaran learned of his father's death. His mother, Liedania, soon thereafter embraced a religious life and, through her son's ministrations, became the first abbess in Ireland. Since she was first cousin to Nadfrach, whose son Aengus became the first Christian king of Cashel, the king was Ciaran's second cousin. And it so happened that Aengus, Liedania and Ciaran would sometimes meet beside the well to organise the conversion of the Irish people.

As Ciaran's monastery grew and prospered, he became a man rich in the possession of herds and fields. Drawing upon the agricultural

St. Ciaran's Cemetery.

learnings of his youth, he built a kingly herd-house, or 'Bovile', which had ten gates and ten special stalls. In each stall each evening were ten heifers. And all the produce from this farm did Ciaran give to the poor and distressed, appropriating nothing for himself the length of his life. He had fifty yoke-horses for the growing of grains, and again he distributed all the harvests to the poor and distressed, nor did he eat wheaten bread his entire life. His daily food, of which he partook only in the evenings, consisted of a mouthful of barley bread, with a dessert of raw herbs and carrageen moss, and a draught of cold well water. His garment was made of deer-skins, bound round with a girdle of untanned hide, and when he rested, his bed was a rock.

St. Ciaran's Pillar Stone.

One day, the steward of the monastery approached Ciaran, and said, "Dear friend, to accommodate our increasing family of monks, we need to add swine to our barn. Shall I go to the market?"

"My friend," replied Ciaran, "you know that the Lord grants us all that we require. We must live in His time."

On the following day, perhaps attracted by the odours from beside the refectory garden, a sow ambled in, littered, and henceforth the monastery had all the stock it needed.

Yet again the steward came to Ciaran and said, "Dear friend, we lack sheep. Should I go and purchase some?"

And Ciaran replied, "He who sent the swine shall present sheep in His time." That very day, on walking out the monastery gate, the steward beheld a flock of twenty-seven sheep grazing. For the rest of his life he felt no need to say a word to anyone, except in prayer.

Many are the accounts of those Ciaran raised from the dead, including his own cousin Aengus, and a band of murdered harpists.

One day in early September of 488, Ciaran spread clean linen over a blackberry bush heavy with fruit. His disciples he asked not to remove the cloth, and the cloth stayed there, secured by the thorns, despite the winds of autumn, the storms of winter. Just after Easter, King Aengus and his queen, Ethnea Huathach, were guests at a nearby castle belonging to Conchyrd, Chieftain of Ossory. Conchyrd prepared a lavish banquet for his distinguished visitors and their retinue. Now during the feast the queen became attracted to the handsome chieftain, and the more she watched him, the more unlawful her passion became. She contrived to tell him of her wish, but he, a man of great integrity, tactfully rejected her advances. Then she conceived a plot. She feigned an illness, knowing that her husband would have to continue on his journey and that she would be left behind in Conchyrd's castle. When asked if there was any remedy for her illness, she replied in a sick whisper, "Blackberries".

Worried as to what would happen if the queen were left behind, Conchyrd hurried to Ciaran. On hearing of the nature of Conchyrd's dilemma, Ciaran collected a measure of the blackberries, which were still ripe under the cloth, and he and Conchyrd delivered them to the queen. Realising that she had to eat them, Ethnea, in the presence of her husband and Conchyrd and Ciaran, took the fruit into her mouth, found the berries delicious, and then discovered that her unlawful passion had disappeared. She began to cry, confessed her crime, and requested absolution. But now Ciaran entered a dilemma. Finally, with a long sigh, he said, "My queen, the Lord has saved thee from a crime by using me as an instrument of your salvation, but I cannot save you from your death impending, for, my daughter, your enemies shall murder yourself and," he turned to his friend Aengus, "the king on the same day, and that shortly." The queen rose, and she and her husband embraced, and continued on their journey. That very year, in 489, Aengus and Ethnea were killed at the battle of Cell Osnadha in the county of Carlow.

Ciaran continued his conversions and healings and prophesying until his death, which some say occurred when he was 360 years old. He died on the very day he had been born, March 5th, and it is thought that whoever celebrates the festival day of his death shall be prosperous in this life, and happy in the next.

For centuries, and up into our own, rounds were paid at the pillar stone on which Ciaran had incised the crosses, and you may still make your rounds on the evening of March 4th, or on March 5th, Saint Ciaran's Day, a holiday celebrated on the island. And beside the stone is Saint Ciaran's holy well. If you listen closely, with love for all God's creatures in your heart, you may occasionally hear the distant tinkle of an ancient bell.

But be careful not to abuse the well. You may drink from it prayerfully, but do not exploit the efficacy of the waters. Once some fisherman drew water from the well, and went off sailing, out to the fertile fishing grounds beside the Fastnet, where the gannets dive and the storm petrels play. Now in their small galley they had a stove, these fishermen, and on this stove they set the water to boil for their tea. But no matter how long they kept their kettle on the fire, the water wouldn't boil. Never again would water boil in that kettle.

To this day, water from St Ciaran's well is employed in the blessing of boats. On the Saint's Feastday, the resident priest draws water from the holy well, and blesses the island's fishing boats and the lifeline to the mainland, the mailboat, the *Naomh Ciaran II*. His prayer, translated from the Latin into Irish, and, here, from Irish into English, may be heard on the afternoon of March 5th once the *Naomh Ciaran II* has come in:

"Lord, listen to our prayers and stretch your right hand over these boats to put your blessing on them. Bless all who sail in them as you blessed Noah and his family in the Ark. Bless the crews as you blessed the apostles, Peter, Andrew, James and John while they were in their boats on the Sea of Galilee. Send your angel from heaven to guard all who use these boats, to help them and to keep them safe from all harm. Amen."

On the Eve of the Feastday, Rosary and Night Prayers are said at the Grotto, followed by Exposition of the Blessed Sacrament in the Oratory. On the holyday itself, at 8:00 a.m., matins are said beside St. Ciaran's Well; and at 10:00 there's a Solemn Sung Mass in the Chapel. No wonder, then, that St. Ciaran is called *Primogenitus Sanctorum Hiberniae*.

Chapter Eighteen
Walking

... the terrain south of the ridge-line is uninhabited, severe, disconcertingly open to non-human immensities, while the northern flank of the island is at least raggedly shawled with the human presence. In fact over parts of the north the fabric of history is so closely woven that it can be as oppressive as the more elemental spaciousness of the south ....

Tim Robinson's *Stones of Aran, Pilgrimage*, 1986

Religion is a way of walking, not a way of talking.

W.R. Inge, Dean of St. Paul's

Cape offers the hiker and the nature lover a visual feast. From the higher knolls of the island, such as Quarantine Hill, the highest elevation at 533 feet above sea level, you see a smorgasbord of seascapes and landscapes. Indeed, from this location you can behold all topographic divisions of the island, the north and the south, the east and the west, and they're delicious!

From Quarantine Hill, a hop skip and a jump north of the windmills, and accessible by a tractor-rutted road, let's take a look around, orient ourselves, and place our order. To the northeast lies Sherkin Island with its several wide sandy strands. Cape's fortunate it hasn't such beaches on any scale, for I can imagine it might then be overrun by myriad sun-and-sand worshippers, just as periodically it's overrun by brazen rabbits. Sherkin's a kind of sister island to Cape, but since she's only a ten-minute shuttle-boat run from the mainland, she lacks Cape's rugged isolation and doesn't require the ritual sea-journey.

Just over the higher hills on Sherkin you can see the top of Baltimore's Beacon, Lot's Wife. To the east lies Kedge Island; on a clear day you can mark the Stags, ten miles off; and on a crystal-clear day you can make out Galley Head, 25 miles distant. Seven Heads and the Old Head of Kinsale are out of sight because of the ocean's curvature, or because Quarantine Hill doesn't tower to 1000 feet!

To the south lies the immensity of the sea, broken by the passage of seabirds, whale and dolphin and porpoise, sunfish and shark, and ships, for three miles out runs the Inshore Traffic Lane. Quite a variety

The Old Lighthouse and Signal Tower.

of vessels pass, and many's the time I've raced for a grandstand seat above Cape's southern coast to observe some of the monsters, mermaids, and marvels that power by, usually east to west: cruise ships, tankers, coasters, container ships, tall ships, cargo ships, supertankers, a fleet of deep-throated destroyers, their engines rumbling almost below hearing range over Cape's patchwork fields. Once, as if in a dream, I saw a high-prowed Viking craft, but I fear a facsimile. Another time I saw three tall ships within half a mile of each other and felt as if I were in the middle of the nineteenth century. And when it's time for the world-famous Fastnet Race, I scuttle like a South Harbour velvet crab up above the Bullig, or over to the Blananarragaun, to a front row seat amid the fields of bell and ling heather interspersed with the prickliest of gorse, or, as some know it, furze.

To the west stands the solitary Fastnet Rock and its towering Lighthouse, recently fully automated, recently demythologised. In severe storms, even the tip of the Fastnet is obscured from Cape by the scud and foam of mighty breakers. When foggy or misty, Fastnet's identifiable foghorn kicks in, a comforting sound and focal point from anywhere on the island as visibility approaches zero. At night its bright flash of rotating light gently and reassuringly sweeps over Cape at five-second intervals as recognisable to mariners as station identifications to radio listeners.

To the north lie Long Island Bay and Roaringwater Bay with its Hundred

Wall below Old Lighthouse.

100

A Ballyieragh path.

Isles. Most obvious are the three Calf Islands, but one can learn to differentiate Goat Island, Long Island, Castle Island, Horse Island, Hare Island. What makes the northern view spectacular, to my mind, are the rising tiers of mountains in West Cork and Kerry. With its radar tracking stations and military installations Mount Gabriel, salient behind Schull, is the closest. Going back further you come upon Seefin, and, back to the most distant range, you come to the Slieve Miskish and Caha mountains, with the long Maulin and the majestic dimpled Hungry Hill, standing proud at 2251 feet and often capped with snow during the winter months. A little to the east you can discern some of the mountains of Kerry.

What I like most about the mountains is the subtle celerity with which they change hue, depending upon the clouds, the time of day, the wind direction (a southeasterly, for example, usually lessens visibility), the chiaroscuro, and, sometimes, what Leonardo called *sfumato*. I can remember standing spellbound for hours, back in the late sixties, staring out to sea while visiting the mainland Temple of Poseidon at Sounion, Greece, and thinking that I had never seen such interplay of light on sea, scattered islands, distant mountains. At sunset, on a summer's day, looking to the north from Quarantine Hill, or from O'Driscoll's Castle, or countless other spots on Cape, I could as easily be beside that Temple of Poseidon. But Oileán Chléire's not boiling in the sun, we have new plantations of lodgepole pine instead of olive trees, and calamaries aren't on today's menu.

Restored by the grand view, let's return to the road and head, well, where my druthers take us. I'm drawn to peer around at intimate detail, and hope that you'll join me. Let's consider the dry stone walls. As Alen MacWeeney and Richard Conniff, in their beautifully photographed book *The Stone Walls of Ireland*, write, "The walls look as though they have been there forever: mottled with lichen and bearded with moss; woven together with vines, hedges, and trees; running, in more than one place, straight across a shallow stream [or disappearing into Cape's Lough Errul, which you'll visit on another walk], as if the wall were there before the water; emerging, in other places, from the low tide mark, as if the walls splashed ashore with the first settlers in Ireland, 8,000 years ago." Roughly 1600 walled fields on Cape attest to mankind's indefatigable toiling spirit and create a patchwork effect on which that same shifting sunlight and ghostly moonlight play.

While the walls help communicate an impression of a singular island character, they have varied, and sometimes multiple, personalities. Here, look, along the entire length of a field, the stone has been placed vertically, there, in the adjoining field, horizontally; this wall is composed of small flat-edged horizontal stones interspersed every ten feet by massive vertical stones; the lower four feet of that wall was built with meticulous care, and then someone added a sloppy layer (the wall's personality undergoes a distinct change); then yet another person added a third layer of large stones, his tractor-pulled plough having sunk more deeply in the field where his predecessors or forebears had laboured with teams of horses.

Over there are walls four, even five feet thick. Often you'll notice that these walls have been filled with small stones, mere inches in diameter, and when time, or a cow scratching its neck, or a careless hiker dislodges one of the critical outside stones, a stretch of wall collapses in an avalanche. What a second of unwitting carelessness releases can require a day's work to rebuild.

With that caveat imbedded in this walk, and with the responsibility to re-shut every gate recognised, and the imperative to watch out for bulls clear, I feel a bit easier about walking with you alongside the hundreds of miles of Cape's variegated treasure troves, for many's the old implement that's tucked away inside or on top of a wall. Frugal islanders have used walls not only for their tired equipment and refuse. Over there you see incorporated into a wall the sides of an old cabin: occasionally you notice the lintel of a window with the window itself plugged, or you spy large rectangular flat stones, one atop the other, in a straight vertical line demarking what was once the jamb of a doorway. And infrequently, but often enough, you come upon a megalithic stone, a stone with putative ogham markings (or old plough marks) inscribed on it, that has been removed from a field and utilised in a wall. So are the mighty not so much fallen as defrocked and re-employed.

I need to rest for a moment, if you don't mind. Some of these hills make me lose my breath, and give me a ferocious appetite. Let's have our picnic lunch and be mental travellers for a bit.

Scattered throughout the island run boreens, both straight and winding, from five to twelve feet wide. There's one to the north of us. Now that only two dozen farmers work areas once tilled by several hundred, a number of the picturesque and formerly well-trodden boreens no longer serve a purpose and have become impenetrable tangles of bramble, bracken, and gorse, perfect nesting ground and cover for birds, including recently introduced pheasants. When the boreens come to an end, and then, often, arable land comes to an end, the walls tend to become lower and lower, sometimes barely three feet high, and they also become thinner, down to the width of a single stone. Such walls are a sure sign of scrub land and are normally furthest from human habitation and closest to the sea.

On the north/northeast side of the island, worthy walls run down to the very edge of the cliffs, because the land remains arable, or at least usable, to where grass gives way to sea-washed rock; but to the south and west the walls generally stop a few hundred yards in from the sea, often at or near the crest of the land as it slopes up before the sharp descent to surf. Because of the exposure of this land to wind and salt, much is covered with heather and gorse, with the occasional burst of ragwort, and is fairly useless to the farmer, unless he or she is into bees, or goats, or, what has not yet happened but which several farmers are currently investigating, deer. To the hiker and nature lover this scrub land's ideal, as long as one is careful of slippery grass and wet stone, of edges or banks that might give way. A decade back, on a steep hillside, all that was found of a young hiker who slipped was a paper bag full of mushrooms and blackberries. Indeed, the cliffs, like the sea itself, have taken their toll of islanders and visitors alike. Beware any track, but especially a rabbit track, above a cliff. Cliffs tell no stories.

Generally speaking, a sturdy walker, with permission from landowners, can circumambulate Cape, staying on the cattle or human track closest to the sea, in two leisurely days. As the hooded crow flies, Cape may be only three miles long by a mile wide. But as the hiker searches for gaps in fences, climbs stiles, scrambles up and down rugged hills, and stops to observe a grey seal, who has already been observing you, or a herd of common porpoise, or, if lucky, a school of killer whales (Cape is near a migration route), or a family of sea otters, "waterdogs" locally, or Risso's Dolphin, then what looks like a short walk on the map becomes a long and pleasant idyll.

Look up from almost any wall and you'll see the sea. From here, with the townland of Killickaforavane in front of us, we see the sea on three sides. Gazing casually, relaxedly out to the south I find particularly resting and hypnotic, and along Cape's rugged coast there are plenty of fine places to stretch out and gawk at immensity. Birdwatchers tell me, however, that concentrating through their telescopes and binoculars out into the distant reaches in expectation of birds that don't materialise is mentally exhausting rather than relaxing. But since they are so regularly rewarded not only with various seabirds, but also with dolphin or a minke whale, or a thirty-foot basking shark cruising placidly only several yards from the bottoms of cliffs, they don't complain.

Stile on Mass Path (Photo by Kate Sawyer).

Usually I prefer a seascape that has land in it. From near O'Driscoll's Castle I look up and marvel at the sheerest, most dramatic cliff on Cape, the Ardacuslaun Cliff, and realise that I don't have to visit Moher. Or if I'm out at the most western tip, the Bill, Pointanardatruha, I gaze south to where the waves crash not only on jagged rocks and cliff but where there are more deep inlets, fjord-like, than anywhere else on

Cape, which cause roiling seas and thick foam to pour in and out of the narrow canyons, foam of such a creamy off-white texture that I imagine shipwrecked barrels of Guinness smashed against nearby stacks.

Aren't you thirsty?

Cape also has blowholes. I wonder at the boulders blasted out of them, loose boulders weighing tons, proof of pounding mountainous fifteen-meter waves. And Cape has caves. Some of them, like fissures in the earth, are said to be Bronze Age mines; others, especially those created by wave power, burrow deep into the bowels of the land. On my farm one cave, entered only from the sea, burrows into the land over one hundred yards. To paddle into this cave (which my elder son and I visited in Chapter 16) at low tide, I still find a harrowing experience. It's as though, once one's penetrated into its depths, anything could happen and no one would be the wiser; unbidden, in a chthonic darkness out of childhood, come fantasies of the freak wave roaring in, melodramatically squashing me the naive interloper against the jagged ceiling. Sounds are eerily amplified, the slightest droplet of water from the roof ringing out as it hits the sea behind my back. I'm always relieved to return to sunlight.

For those with less thirst for adventure, like me after I finally rocket out of that spooky but alluring cave in South Harbour, an easy walk up the road through the Glen to the Old Lighthouse does wonders for the spleen. Shall we walk off this double repast of picnic and view while we paradoxically take in more? Shall we stroll down to North Harbour and have some homemade goat's milk ice-cream, the best ice-cream I've found in Ireland?

Ah, now that we're feeling energetic, shall we walk up the Lacavuar, the longest, steepest road on the island, with a higher gradient than any road I remember from my walks in the Alps? Island

farmers haul loaded trailers up this hill with their tractors, but I notice that most island women, and some island men, sensibly avoid driving up the hill altogether. And some avoid going down it, taking the

Stone wall.

long detour to North Harbour from "over east" by turning at "the cross" (the major crossroads) and then down the long slowly descending hill past the post office, down by the school and the priest's house, and along South Harbour, the "Bullaun Road", the way we returned from our morning walk. Sobering, I confess, are the stories of brakes giving out on the Lacavuar. While the birdwatchers call this road the A 1, a Baltimorean yachtsman who regularly visits Cape refers to it as "Faith Hill": faith is required to make it to the heavenly top and the nearby church.

Once at the top of the Lacavuar, from which we can look almost straight down onto North Harbour, we could cut south, into the rocky deserted townland named the Keenleen, which commandingly overlooks the unspoilt South Harbour as well as Roaringwater Bay. Or if you'd prefer a long easy walk, we could continue way over east and visit the most famous of Cape's "Galláns", or standing stones, which here include the marriage stone, where, as Liam Ó Loideoin writes in *Walkers Guide to Cape Clear Island*, "… couples plighted troth by shaking hands through the aperture". (I can only add that the couples must have had mighty small hands.) In early pre-Christian times, he relates, "The couple were married [here] in the presence of the Pagan King."

After visiting the standing stones, we might follow the lane down to Foilcoagh, the Cove of the Cuckoos, now disused, and delightfully free of human sound for such a naturally protected harbour. Close to Sherkin, it once was a place of constant activity. It's here that the ESB tentatively plans to run an electrical submarine cable ashore, following late in the wake of the 1853 submarine telegraph cable.

If we're still raring to go after visiting the tranquillity of Foilcoagh, and especially if it's spring, with a gentle breeze and quiet swells, we could walk the track down to Coosanvaud, a tiny unprotected harbour. Covering the rocks is the powerfully yellow Xanthoria (a common lichen you will notice in many places on Cape, and which was once thought to be a cure for jaundice). Yellow-flowering, sweet-smelling kidney vetch and purple-pink thrift ("sea pinks") bloom just above the rocks, the sea as backdrop. I imagine this scene as quietly, perfectly arranged as a Zen garden.

On the way home from this imagined walk, we could cut in behind the church and tread the Mass Path. This public right of way requires, like the roads, no permission. With its many stiles and quiet views of the Old Lighthouse, the Glen, Ballyieragh, South Harbour, and the Fastnet, the Mass Track offers an easy short-cut from places such as the church, the museum, one of the Irish summer colleges, to places south, including the post office. In the summer, lines of single-file Irish college students may be seen gaily tripping, or despondently splashing, along this gentle gradient, which connects where they live in the Glen to where they study in Lissamona.

Somewhere near the southern end of the Mass Path the Cape Clear Stone, with its finely carved spirals and zigzags, was discovered. I gave its story in Chapter 3. Responding to our stone's three spirals, one above the other, surrounded by zigzags, I read some scholarship: "The separation of a formless unity into two reciprocal principles which generate a third and form the multiplicity of creation is a universal and archaic cosmological idea. In sky imagery the sun and moon represent the two opposite principles and the stars represent multiplicity. Together they make up time and space and the entire universe. The megalithic artist apparently viewed the multiplicity of the stars and the multiplicity of the 'world' below as originating from the same source, and both are seen to conform to basic geometrical structures."

What? That put you to sleep, a siesta? No further walk? But don't you want to visit the Old Lighthouse? The freshwater lake? The pounding surf to the southwest? The castle? Ah, you just want to put your feet up here and observe all the comings and goings at North Harbour. Oh, you've decided to stay for a week instead of a day. Good decision.

Well then, good-bye. Good luck to ye! Maybe we'll meet at the small sandy beach called Coosaneska tomorrow!

Back home, at our sitting-place, I too put up my feet on a stone, sit on a stone, and overlook inner and outer harbours. Beside me is a patch of cat's ears, waving their dandelion-like heads. By a stone shed behind me grows a bed of Joseph's ladder or cock's comb. Along the driveway fuchsia springs out of the stone wall. From the wall beside me emerges a single spire of pennywort or navelwort, and waving in the breeze between me and the view I like most in the world is a single stately spear of purple-belled foxglove.

I may be pooped, but already I'm looking forward to tomorrow's ramble. In fact, I'm growing downright hungry.

Chapter Nineteen
Values in the Wind

The world is charged with the grandeur of God.
Gerard Manly Hopkins, "God's Grandeur"

W hy have two American ex-teachers moved not just to Ireland but to a remote island outpost like Clear Island? At 52 and 55, we're lucky enough, healthy enough, to be able to search for a quality of life rather than a standard of living. On Cape we find what we most value and what we've most lacked: freedom, community, nature. A freedom to be ourselves; an intermingling community that has to be fairly self-reliant — there's no one else to help within easy reach other than the Baltimore lifeboat; a nature of which one is continuously aware and which emphasises elemental experience.

And I mean elemental, for on this sea-girt speck of rocky outcropping one is at all times intensely aware of the weather: there's no escaping it, whether in pub conversation or on a cliff top, whether out fishing or in the sacrosanct bowels of a house, by which in our case I mean a parlour with one little window toward the sheltered south. Yet even in this tiny room, with stone walls two and a half feet thick, there's no full release from the wind: it comes down the chimney with the coal smoke, or howls through the shrubbery in the yard, or eerily and piercingly whines about the eaves like a levitated sick hound.

I now appreciate why most religions have recognised wind as divine energy. No wonder the Old Testament Jehovah was linked to whirlwinds, that the ancient Greeks had their Aeolus. God's breath was spirit, spirit was wind.

On Cape there's no shortage of wind, especially once halcyon summer's gone. Wind engineers reckon that if Cape had a renewed and enhanced windmill farm with three wind turbines instead of the present proven two, and if Cape were connected to the mainland grid, the island could export sufficient energy through the winter months, when its own diminished population's needs are slight and the mainland's needs are at their peak, so that over the course of a year it could produce two to three times the amount of energy it itself could use. Except for the whooshing noise of the windmills, this energy would be pollution-free. What an apt way to put a renewable resource to use.

Nell in a Force 10

When there's no wind one has to beware the trap and think ahead. Outdoors you learn to place heavy stones onto all kinds of objects: an outdoor table or chair, a sheet of tin, an extra slate, a piece of plastic sheeting, a bucket. Indoors you learn not to open a door on one side of the house when a door is open on the other side, otherwise a simple door becomes a lethal force. You learn to plant the more sensitive vegetables and flowers in the shelter of a wall. You learn to park your car with its engine in the lee, and thus out of the salt-laden moisture-carrying breeze. Your clothes-line becomes a clothes-rope, your clothes-pole becomes

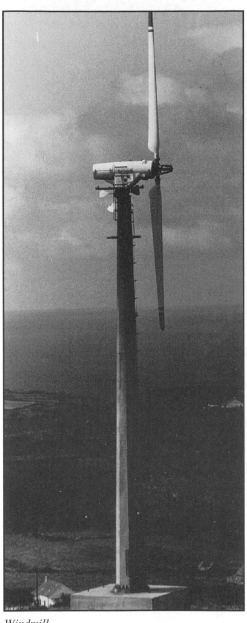

Windmill.

as strong as a mast. You don't leave home without securing your windows, even wedging them in the winter against vibration. Neighbours speak of walking at a 45 degree tilt for months.

Sometimes I feel as though I could eat the wind. It blows so fresh, smells so good, whether it's just come over a stretch of heather, or through a patch of kidney vetch, or arrived directly off the sea. When it's coming from the south, or the west, it's been free of new pollution for thousands of miles. As with a good wine, certain winds have a bouquet. Most east winds I'd give back to the wind steward.

When I ask Nell what she particularly values about Cape, she doesn't hesitate: "Blackberries [not St. Ciaran's, thank you], wind, walks, cliffs, waves, sea, friendly people; you're curious about the sea and then you discover the seals have been curious about you; hauling lobster pots; uncomfy with conger eels in a boat; legs torn by gorse; a look out to sea in the morning instead of an alarm clock; time to bake a loaf of bread both for us and for those who drop by; the sound of wind when it keeps you awake at night; the excitement of house-high waves; going to church now and then (even though we're not Catholics); the freedom, the chance, to become a private person without a society expecting you to do certain things. *Before,*"she adds, *"responsibilities and commitments interfered with living; here they contribute to living. There's honesty in life here, and individual lives take on meaning. Here we have a convert's joy."*

Having ambushed her, and seen wind turn up in various guises, I wonder about myself, what I value. I discover that Cape makes my life an adventure rather than, as all too often before, a routine, an ordeal. There's a magic about living on such an island, something deep and ineffable, something filled with God's wind. As my favorite poet Hopkins said, and as Cape helps me regularly realise, "There lives the dearest freshness deep down things."

DOLPHIN MEMORY

walking cross-country
single file
along the cattle paths
through the belling heather
down, down to the sea, to the Bullig,
we happened upon a hidden dell
hummocky with cushions of grass,
riddled with rabbit warrens,
we alone above
the nesting ground of the wild-crying circling
oystercatcher,
his brilliant orange beak as brightly piercing as
his cries

my daughter, my wife, me, no soul else,
it seemed,
oh we lay back chatting
about, well, things, us
children's literature, conger eels,
the time we pitched our tent
in the Vendée, filled the VW bus with shells

when exploding from the sea below,
came a snort of snorts

we jumped into each other

there, hanging in the air,
the majesty of dolphin,
the static middle of a ballerina leap,
giving us a startling reminder of the deep

arced down into the sea, rose
into another leap,
danced across the harbour's mouth,
disappearing into distance

that snort that afternoon
hallowed the air,

hallows it still

SELECTED BIBLIOGRAPHY

Burke, J. M., "Cape Clear Island", *Journal of the Cork Historical and Archaeological Society*, Vol. XIV, 2nd Series, 1908

Conlon, J. P., "Cape Clear Island", *Journal of the Cork Historical and Archaeological Society*, Vol. XXIV, No. 118, April-June 1918

De Paor, Liam, *Saint Patrick's World*, Four Courts Press, Dublin, 1993

Donovan, Daniel, *Sketches in Carbery*, McGlashan & Gill, Dublin, 1876

Feehan, John M. *The Wind that round the Fastnet sweeps*, Mercier Press, Cork, 1978

Gunn, Marion, *Céad Fáilte go Cléire*, An Clóchomhar, Baile Atha Cliath, 1990

Hogan, John, *St. Ciaran, Patron of Ossory*, "Journal" Office, Kilkenny, 1876

Holland, Rev. W., *History of West Cork and the Diocese of Ross*, Skibbereen, 1949

Lewis, Samuel, *A Topographical Dictionary of Ireland*, S. Lewis & Co., London, 1837

Lockley, Ronald M., *Flight of the Storm Petrel*, David & Charles, London, ca. 1982

MacWeeney, Alen, and Conniff, Richard, *The Stone Walls of Ireland*, Thames & Hudson, London, 1986

Mulcahy, Rev. D. B., *Life of S. Kiaran (The Elder) of Seir*, Gill & Son, Dublin, 1895

Newby, Eric, *Round Ireland in Low Gear*, Picador, London, 1987

O Céadagáin, Domhnall, "Sentimental Voyage: St. Kieran, Cape Clear and Fr. O'Halloran", 1992

O'Hanlon, Rev. John, *Lives of the Irish Saints*, Duffy & Sons, Dublin, late nineteenth century

O'Leary, Patrick J., "A Passage Tomb on Clear Island in West Cork?", *Journal of the Cork Historical and Archaeological Society*, Volume XCIV, No. 253, 1989

O Loideoin, Liam, *Walkers Guide to Cape Clear Island*, Comharchumann Chléire Teo, Skibbereen, 1989

O Síocháin, Conchúr, *The Man from Cape Clear*, (trans. by Riobárd P. Breatnach), Mercier Press, Cork, 1975

Rousmaniere, John, *"Fastnet Force 10"*, W.W. Norton & Company, New York and London, 1980

Scott, C.W., *History of the Fastnet Rock Lighthouse*, Schull Books,

Co Cork, 1906, facsimile reissued 1993

Sharrock, J. T. R., editor, *The Natural History of Cape Clear*, T. & A. D. Poyser, Berkhamstead, 1973

Smith, Charles, *The Ancient and Present State of the County and City of Cork*, Cork, 1700's

Somerville-Large, Peter, *The Coast of West Cork*, Appletree Press, Belfast, 1972

The Grand Irish Tour, Penguin Books, Middlesex, 1982

Townsend, H., *General and Statistical Survey of the County of Cork.* ..., 2nd Edition, Edwards & Savage, Dublin, 1815

Wilson, R., Jr., "A Brief Description of Cape Clear", Dublin, 1834

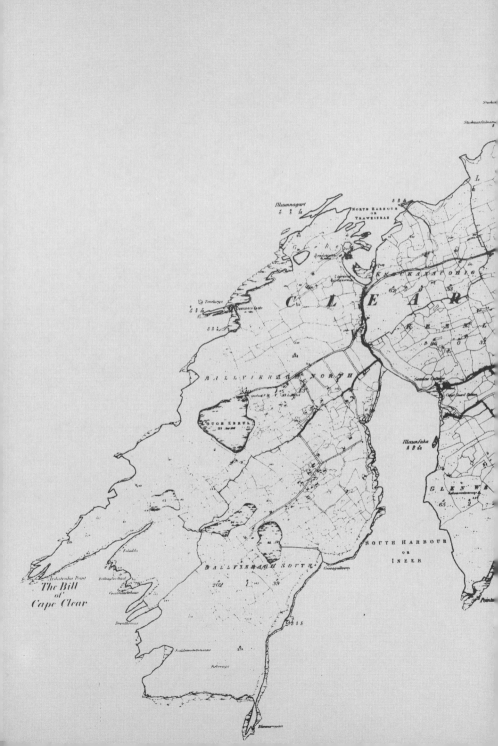